THE BABYLONIAN GENESIS

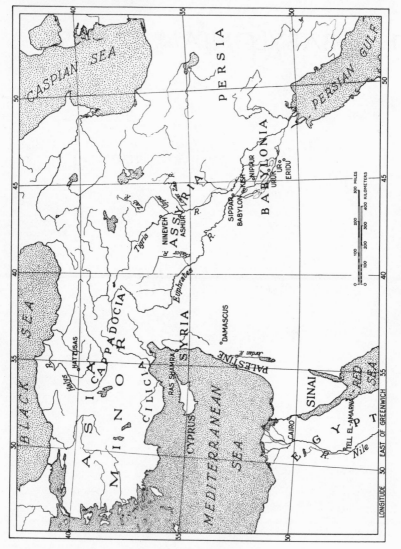

A map of the ancient Near East

THE BABYLONIAN GENESIS

The Story of Creation

ALEXANDER HEIDEL

Second Edition

THE UNIVERSITY OF CHICAGO PRESS

CHICAGO & LONDON

THE UNIVERSITY OF CHICAGO PRESS, CHICAGO 60637
The University of Chicago Press, Ltd., London

International Standard Book Number: 0-226-32399-4

Library of Congress Catalog Card Number: 51-822

80 79 78 77 76   13 12 11 10 9

PREFACE

THE excavations which during the last one hundred years or more have been carried on in Egypt, Palestine, Babylonia, Assyria, and other lands of the ancient Orient have opened up vistas of history that were undreamed of before the archeologist with his spade appeared upon the scene. They have furnished us with a remarkable background for the Old Testament; they have shown with singular clarity that the story of the ancient Hebrews, politically speaking, is but an episode in a gigantic drama in which such peoples as the Egyptians, Babylonians, and Assyrians played the chief roles; they have shown that the Old Testament is not an isolated body of literature but that it has so many parallels in the literature of the nations surrounding Israel that it is impossible to write a scientific history of the Hebrews or a scientific commentary on the Old Testament without at least a fair knowledge of the history and the literature of Israel's neighbors.

This is true particularly with regard to the records from Babylonia and Assyria. So numerous are the points of contact between the Old Testament and the inscriptions found in these two countries that whole books have been written on this very subject. Again and again the annals of the Assyrian monarchs confirm, elucidate, or supplement the Hebrew chronicles of Judah and Israel, while the creation and flood stories of the Babylonians as well as the Code of Hammurabi abound in striking parallels to the corresponding portions of the Old Testament.

The present volume deals with one group of these parallels; it is concerned with the creation stories of Babylonia and the problem of their relation to our Old Testament literature. This little study is intended primarily not for the professional Assyriologist but rather for the Old Testament scholar and the Christian minister. Consonant with this purpose, it has been my aim throughout to make the meaning of the texts stand out as clearly as possible, to reduce to a minimum all linguistic discus-

v

sions of the Babylonian material, and to confine myself to things that will really be of help and interest to those who have been intrusted with the office of expounding the sacred truths enshrined in Holy Writ.

The present edition constitutes an almost complete revision of the previous one. I have retranslated all the cuneiform texts and have considerably altered and enlarged the rest of the book. There are but few pages on which no change has been made. In the revision of the cuneiform stories I enjoyed the unstinted co-operation of Associate Professor F. W. Geers and also had the pleasure of discussing a number of problems with Professor Benno Landsberger. It is hardly necessary to add that, as a member of the Assyrian Dictionary staff of the Oriental Institute of the University of Chicago, I had full access to the Dictionary files, for which the present translation of the cuneiform texts has been prepared. For the illustrative material I am indebted to the British Museum and to the Oriental Institute. Special acknowledgments are given in the List of Illustrations. The publication of this material has been made possible through a subvention from the Committee on Allocation of Funds for Scholarly Research of The Lutheran Church—Missouri Synod, for which I am sincerely grateful.

If those for whom this volume is primarily intended will find it helpful in their work or in the solution of some personal problems, I shall feel amply repaid for the efforts expended upon it.

ALEXANDER HEIDEL

ORIENTAL INSTITUTE
UNIVERSITY OF CHICAGO

TABLE OF CONTENTS

LIST OF ILLUSTRATIONS

LIST OF SYMBOLS AND SPECIAL CHARACTERS

( ) in translations inclose elements not in the original but desirable or necessary for a better understanding in English.

(?) indicate that the meaning is uncertain.

[ ] inclose restorations in the text.

⌈ ⌉ inclose a word, a phrase, or a line which is partially damaged.

.... (1) in translations indicate that the text is unintelligible to the translator;

(2) in titles of books indicate omission.

[. . . .] or ⌈. . . .⌉ indicate that the text is wholly or partially damaged and therefore unintelligible.

‾ or ^ indicates a long vowel.

˘ indicates a short vowel.

ʾ = א.

ʿ = ע.

ḫ = ח.

ṣ = צ.

ś = שׂ.

ṭ = ט.

ix

CHAPTER I

ENÛMA ELISH

O F ALL the Semitic inscriptions composed in cuneiform writing few have awakened as great a general interest as the epic known among the Babylonians and Assyrians as *Enûma elish* ("When above"), which takes its name from the opening words of the poem. Aside from linguistic considerations, this widespread popularity of *Enûma elish* is in part due to its great significance for the study of the theogonic and cosmogonic views of the Mesopotamians, and thus for a comparative study of ancient Near Eastern religion in general; but above all else it is due to the fact that *Enûma elish* presents quite a number of analogies to the first two chapters of the Book of Genesis.

THE DISCOVERY OF THE TABLETS

This great epic is recorded on seven clay tablets and covers in all a little over one thousand lines. The first fragments to come to light were discovered by Austen H. Layard, Hormuzd Rassam, and George Smith among the ruins of King Ashurbanipal's (668–*ca.* 630 B.C.) great library at Nineveh between the years 1848 and 1876. During their explorations at Ashur (the old capital of Assyria), from 1902 to 1914, the German excavators unearthed a number of fragments of an Assyrian version of the Babylonian story (especially of Tablets I, VI, and VII) which differs from the latter chiefly in that some copies substitute the name of Ashur, the king of the Assyrian gods, for that of Marduk, the king of the Babylonian deities, and in that they make Laḫmu and Laḫâmu the parents of Ashur. In 1924–25 two almost complete tablets, I and VI, of a Neo-Babylonian version of the epic were discovered at Kish by the joint expedition of Oxford University and the Field Museum of Chicago. And in 1928–29 the Germans found quite a large Neo-Babylonian fragment of Tablet VII at Uruk (the biblical Erech).

1

Thanks to these discoveries and to purchases of fragments which have been made from dealers in antiquities (the provenance of most of these fragments being uncertain), the epic has been restored almost in its entirety; the only tablet of which a large portion is still wanting is Tablet V.

THE PUBLICATION OF THE MATERIAL

The first to publish an account of the epic was George Smith, of the British Museum, who in 1875 described in a letter to the *Daily Telegraph* the contents of about twenty fragments of the creation series. In 1876 appeared his book *The Chaldean Account of Genesis*, which contained a translation and discussion of all the pieces which had been identified. All this material was very fragmentary, but the resemblance of its contents to the initial chapters of the Old Testament was unmistakable, and consequently it had an immediate appeal to a much wider circle of students than would otherwise have been the case. Since then this story has been copied and translated by a great many Assyriologists, especially as new tablets or portions of tablets have been found.

In 1890 Peter Jensen, in his work *Die Kosmologie der Babylonier* (Strassburg), published a translation together with a transliteration and a commentary; five years later Heinrich Zimmern issued a new and improved translation in Hermann Gunkel's volume *Schöpfung und Chaos in Urzeit und Endzeit* (Göttingen, 1895); the very next year Friedrich Delitzsch issued *Das babylonische Weltschöpfungsepos* (Leipzig, 1896). Within a few years this was superseded by Jensen's penetrating and still highly valuable study of *Enûma elish* in his book *Assyrisch-babylonische Mythen und Epen* (Berlin, 1900), containing a transliteration, a translation, and an extensive commentary. At the turn of the century, L. W. King issued a large number of creation fragments in his two volumes *The Seven Tablets of Creation* (London, 1902), the first of which contains chiefly transliterations, translations, and discussions, while the second offers cuneiform texts only.

More recent publications dealing with this subject are A. Ungnad, *Die Religion der Babylonier und Assyrer* (Jena, 1921);

Erich Ebeling, *Das babylonische Weltschöpfungslied* in Bruno
Meissner, *Altorientalische Texte und Untersuchungen*, II, 4
(Breslau, 1921); Ebeling's revised rendition in Hugo Gress-
mann's volume *Altorientalische Texte zum Alten Testament* (Ber-
lin and Leipzig, 1926); S. Langdon, *The Babylonian Epic of Cre-
ation* (Oxford, 1923) and *Babylonian Penitential Psalms to
Which Are Added Fragments of the Epic of Creation from Kish*
(Paris, 1927); Sir E. A. Wallis Budge, *The Babylonian Legends of
the Creation* (London, 1931); Anton Deimel, *"Enuma Eliš" und
Hexaëmeron* (Rome, 1934); G. Furlani, *Il Poema della creazione*
(Bologna, 1934); and René Labat, *Le Poème babylonien de la
création* (Paris, 1935).

The publications in which the cuneiform texts have been
made available are for the most part cited in the studies just
mentioned; the rest will be referred to in footnotes in the present
volume.

A SUMMARY OF THE STORY

The epic opens with a brief reference to the time when nothing except the divine parents, Apsû and Ti'âmat, and their son
Mummu existed. Apsû was the primeval sweet-water ocean, and
Ti'âmat the salt-water ocean, while Mummu probably represented the mist rising from the two bodies of water and hovering over them, particularly since in Tablet VII:86 he is brought
in direct relation with the clouds. These three types of water
were mingled in one, forming an immense, undefined mass in
which were contained all the elements of which afterward the
universe was made. As yet, there was neither heaven nor earth,
not even a reed marsh was to be seen. In time, Apsû and Ti'â-
mat brought forth the brother and sister pair Laḫmu and
Laḫâmu. While these two were growing up, another brother and
sister pair came into being, Anshar and Kishar, who surpassed
the older children in stature. The nature of these two divine
pairs is still a matter for conjecture.

After many years, a son was born to Anshar and Kishar.
They named him Anu, probably in allusion to the fact that he
was the likeness of his father, Anshar. Anu was the sky-god.
He, in turn, begot Nudimmud, his likeness. Nudimmud, also
known as Enki and Ea, was a god of exceptional wisdom and

strength; he became the god of the subterranean sweet waters, the god of magic, and the mastermind of the Mesopotamian divinities. He had no rival among his fellow-gods; in fact, because of the advantages with which he was endowed, he was the master even of his fathers.

The younger gods, being full of life and vitality, naturally enjoyed noisy, hilarious gatherings. These, however, caused serious distress to their old, inactive, and rest-loving parents and grandparents, Apsû and Ti'âmat. Peaceful means were tried to diminish the disturbing clamor, but without success. Finally, Apsû, in utter exasperation, resolved on a drastic course of action. Accompanied by Mummu, his son and vizier, he went before Ti'âmat and submitted a plan to her which made her motherly heart cry out in painful rage: "Why should we destroy that which we ourselves have brought forth? Their way is indeed painful, but let us take it good-naturedly!" But Apsû, supported by his vizier, adhered to his expressed purpose with adamant tenacity: "I will destroy (them) and put an end to their way, that silence be established, and then let us sleep!"

At the break of the news, the gods were filled with consternation and ran about aimlessly. Finally, they quieted down and sat in silent gloom, without anyone being able to suggest a way of deliverance. Fortunately, in that dark hour there was found one who was master even of Apsû; it was Ea, "the one of supreme understanding, the skilful, (and) wise," the god of magic. He made a magic circle of some kind around the gods, as a protection against attack, and then composed an overpowering, holy incantation. He recited it and caused it to descend, as a soporific force, upon Apsû. As Ea recited his incantation, Apsû succumbed to the power of the spell and sank into a profound sleep. And as Apsû was lying there, suffused with sleep, Ea removed his royal tiara and his supernatural radiance and clothed himself therewith. After he had thus come into possession of Apsû's might and splendor, he slew the father of all the gods and imprisoned his vizier, gaining his victory chiefly through the application of authority or power inherent in the spoken word, the magic of the spell. Ti'âmat remained unmolested, since she had not been in sympathy with Apsû's designs.

Upon the slain Apsû, Ea subsequently established a spacious abode. He named it "Apsû" and appointed it for shrines for himself and for other deities. There he and his wife, Damkina, dwelt in splendor.

There also it was that Marduk, "the wisest of the gods," was born, the one who was destined some day to deliver the gods from an even more dreadful foe and to become the head of the vast Babylonian pantheon. "He who begot him was Ea, his father. Damki[na], his mother, was she who bore him. He sucked the breasts of goddesses" and thus imbibed additional divine power and qualities. Marduk was an imposing figure, endowed with flashing eye and awe-inspiring majesty. When his father beheld him, "he rejoiced, he beamed, his heart was filled with joy." Evidently by means of magic, Ea then conferred upon his son double equality with the gods, which manifested itself in the two faces of Marduk and the doubled dimensions of his members, so that "he was exalted among the gods."

In the meantime, Tiᵓâmat was disturbed, doubtless because of the violent death of her husband. Day and night, she restlessly moved about. Her restlessness mounted as some of the gods, led by Kingu (cf. Tablet VI:23–30), in their wickedness instigated her to avenge the death of her spouse. Tiᵓâmat yielded and decided on war against the gods who were either responsible for or in sympathy with the murder of her husband.

The rebel gods now publicly seceded and went over to the side of Tiᵓâmat; they raged and plotted, not resting day or night; "they held a meeting and planned the conflict." Tiᵓâmat, on her part, gave birth to eleven kinds of monster serpents and ferocious dragons for the impending contest; she exalted Kingu to be her new spouse, she intrusted him with the high command of the battle, gave him dominion over all the gods, and presented him with the coveted tablet of destinies with all its magic powers. A formidable demonic host had suddenly sprung into existence.

It was not until Tiᵓâmat was almost ready for the assault that someone informed Ea of the imminent peril. When Ea, the wise and skilful, the hero who had vanquished Apsû, heard of the impending danger, he was benumbed with fear and dismay.

When he had thought the matter over and had regained his composure, he went to Anshar, his grandfather, and "communicated to him all that Tiᵇâmat had planned" and the preparations she had made, repeating word for word the report which he himself had received. Anshar was moved to expressions of deepest grief and grave concern and appealed to Ea to proceed against the foe. Ea obeyed the voice of his grandfather, but the venture, though undertaken by him who had achieved such a decisive victory over Apsû, ended in failure. Anshar then turned to his son Anu, urging him to try peaceful measures, saying: "[Go a]nd stand thou before Tiᵇâmat, [that] her spirit [become quiet and] her heart calm down. [If] she does not hearken to thy word, speak our [word(?)] to her, that she may be quieted." Anu went, armed with his own authority and that of the leader of the gods. But, unlike Apsû, Tiᵇâmat could not be overcome by any amount of mere authority or any degree of mere magic power; she had to be conquered through the application of physical force. Anu returned in terror, asking to be relieved of the task. Anshar lapsed into silence, looking upon the ground and shaking his head. "All the Anunnaki were assembled at the place. Their lips were closed, [they sat in] silence." Never before had the gods been in such a plight. The picture is painted in extremely dark and somber colors to make the greatness of the subsequent victory all the more evident.

In this moment of supreme crisis, a happy thought occurred to Anshar; he remembered the prowess of valiant Marduk, who in some way had already proved his valor (cf. Tablet II:95) and who certainly would not fail. Marduk was summoned into the presence of Ea, to be instructed by his father, and then appeared before Anshar. When Anshar saw the young Marduk, abounding in strength and radiating confidence, "his heart was filled with joy; he kissed his lips, his fear was removed," while Marduk assured him: "[Anshar], be not silent, (but) open thy lips; I will go and accomplish all that is in thy heart! [My father, c]reator, be glad and rejoice; soon thou shalt trample upon the neck of Tiᵇâmat!" There was no doubt in anyone's mind that Marduk, despite his youth, could save the gods from their powerful enemy. Moreover, Marduk was ready to go to battle and deliver the gods from disaster. But he demanded a high price—supreme and undisputed authority among the gods. Anshar agreed to the terms (cf. Tablet III:65–66), but the decision had to be confirmed by the gods in their assembly.

Anshar therefore dispatched Kaka, his vizier, to Laḥmu and Laḥâmu and all the other gods who were living at a great distance and, consequently, had as yet no knowledge of the impending struggle. Kaka was to inform the gods of the gravity of the situation and to summon them into the presence of Anshar. After a few prefatory remarks, Anshar gave Kaka a verbatim repetition of the account of Tiʾâmat's hostile activities and charged him to repeat the message word for word to Laḥmu and Laḥâmu. Kaka went and repeated Anshar's speech in every detail.[1] Upon learning of the sudden and unparalleled crisis, the gods were perplexed and horrified, they cried aloud and wailed painfully. They departed and entered into the presence of Anshar, filling the Court of Assembly. They kissed one another as they met, and then sat down to a banquet, which Anshar had prepared to put the gods in the right frame of mind. "The sweet wine dispelled their fears; [their] bod[ies] swelled as they drank the strong drink. Exceedingly carefree were they, their spirit was exalted; for Marduk, their avenger, they decreed the destiny."

After the feast, the gods erected a lordly throne-dais for Marduk, and the young god sat down before his fathers to receive sovereignty. In a solemn speech, the gods conferred upon him the powers of the supreme position in the pantheon and gave him "kingship over the totality of the whole universe." To determine whether Marduk actually had this power, the gods made a test. They placed a garment in their midst. At his command, the garment was destroyed; again at his command, the garment was restored to its former condition. When the gods beheld the efficacy of his word, they rejoiced and paid homage,

[1] The constant verbatim repetition of the description of Tiʾâmat's preparations for war is fully consonant with the style of the Babylonian poets, as we can discern from the Gilgamesh Epic and other literary productions. The same stylistic feature is observable in the epical literature of Ras Shamra (see H. L. Ginsberg in the *Bulletin of the American Schools of Oriental Research*, No. 84 [1941], pp. 12–13).

acclaiming Marduk king of the gods. They invested him with the royal insignia, the scepter, the throne, and the royal robe(?), adding thereto "an irresistible weapon smiting the enemy," with the plea: "Go and cut off the life of Tiᵓâmat!" Marduk departed to prepare for the fray. He made a bow, put an arrowhead on the arrow, and grasped a club in his right hand; the bow and quiver he hung at his side; like the storm-god, he caused lightning to precede him; he filled his body with a blazing flame; he made a net and had the four winds, the gift of Anu, carry it for him; as a further aid, he created seven winds of his own; he raised the rain-flood and mounted his ir-resistible, terrible storm chariot, drawn by four frightful mythological creatures. Clad in a terrifying coat of mail, with an overpowering brightness about his head, and supplied with various apotropaic means, Marduk then set out to meet the seemingly invincible Tiᵓâmat, the gods milling around him.

The mere appearance of Marduk, arrayed in all his terrifying might and dazzling splendor, threw Kingu and his helpers into confusion. Tiᵓâmat alone remained unperturbed, greeting Mar-duk with awful taunts and apparently a loud roar to frighten the youthful god. But Marduk was of tougher fiber than his father Ea and his grandfather Anu. Without being in the least disturbed, he denounced Tiᵓâmat in trenchant terms for her wicked measures and challenged her to a duel! "When Tiᵓâmat heard this, she became like one in a frenzy (and) lost her reason. She cried out loud (and) furiously," shaking to her very foun-dations! But she accepted the challenge, and the two pressed on to single combat. Marduk spread out his net and enmeshed her. "When Tiᵓâmat opened her mouth to devour him, he drove in the evil wind, in order that (she should) not (be able) to close her lips." As the raging winds distended her body, Marduk shot an arrow through her open mouth; it struck her heart and de-stroyed her life. Having thus killed Tiᵓâmat, he cast down her carcass and victoriously stood upon it. When her followers saw that their leader was dead, they dispersed and tried to flee. But none escaped.

The enemy gods were imprisoned and deprived of their

weapons. Marduk took from Kingu the tablet of destinies, sealed it with his own seal, to prove his ownership and to legalize his claim to it, and fastened it on his breast. After having strengthened his hold upon the captive gods, he returned to Ti°âmat, split her skull with his unsparing club, cut her arteries, and caused the north wind to carry her blood southward to out-of-the-way places. Finally, he divided the colossal body of Ti°âmat into two parts to create the universe. With one half of her corpse he formed the sky, with the other he fashioned the earth, and then established Anu, Enlil, and Ea in their respective domains.

Next, he created stations in the sky for the great gods; he organized the calendar, by setting up stellar constellations to determine, by their rising and setting, the year, the months, and the days; he built gates in the east and in the west for the sun to enter and to depart; in the very center of the sky he fixed the zenith; he caused the moon to shine forth and intrusted the night to her. After some detailed orders to the moon, the tablet dealing with the creation and organization of the heavenly bodies breaks off.

The imprisoned gods, who had joined the ranks of Ti°âmat, were made the servants of the victors, for whose sustenance they had to provide. However, their menial task proved so burdensome that they asked Marduk for relief. As Marduk listened to the words of the captive gods, he resolved to create man and to impose on him the service which the defeated deities had to render. In consultation with Ea, it was then decided to kill the ringleader of the rebels, to create mankind with his blood, and to set the captive gods free. In a solemn court Kingu was indicted. He it was who "created the strife," who "caused Ti°âmat to revolt and prepare for battle." Accordingly, Kingu was bound and brought before Ea. With the aid of certain gods, Ea severed his arteries and created mankind with his blood, acting on the ingenious plans of Marduk. Man now had to take over the work of the defeated army of gods and feed the host of Babylonian divinities.

Next, Marduk divided the totality of the Anunnaki, a name

which in the early period seems to have been a general designation for all the gods of heaven and earth. Marduk set three hundred of them in the heavens, and three hundred he assigned to the earth, allotting to each group their appropriate tasks.

As a token of gratitude for their deliverance at the hands of Marduk, the Anunnaki built the city of Babylon and Marduk's great temple Esagila with its stagetower. Then the gods, after a joyful banquet, in solemn assembly, recited the fifty names of Marduk. As the gods had previously met in the Court of Assembly to invest Marduk with supreme regal power and authority before he set out against Ti'âmat, so they were gathered again in the same place to confer upon him fifty titles with all the attributes and abilities of the various gods of the pantheon, thus making "his way pre-eminent," in further appreciation of all that Marduk had done.

The poem closes with an epilogue urging the people to study these names, to hold them in remembrance, and to rejoice in Marduk, that it may be well with them.[2]

THE OBJECT OF THE EPIC

Enûma elish is the principal source of our knowledge of Mesopotamian cosmology. While the various other creation stories treat of certain aspects of the cosmos, *Enûma elish* gives us an account of the origin and the order of the universe as a whole. The universe, in its component parts, begins with the gods, who represent cosmic elements or forces in nature (although the character of some of the gods is still uncertain), and is organized and completed through the creative activities of Marduk, the author of the present world order.

Yet, *Enûma elish* is not primarily a creation story at all. If we were to put together all the lines which treat of creation, including the theogony and even granting that most of the missing portion of Tablet V deals with works of creation, they would cover not even two of the seven tablets but only about as much space as is devoted to Marduk's fifty names in Tablets VI and VII. The brief and meager account of Marduk's acts of crea-

---

[2] This summary has benefited to some degree from Thorkild Jacobsen's observations in Frankfort, Wilson, Jacobsen, and Irwin, *The Intellectual Adventure of Ancient Man* (Chicago, 1947), pp. 170–83.

tion is in sharp contrast to the circumstantial description of
his birth and growth, his preparations for battle, his conquest
of Tiʾâmat and her host, and the elaborate and pompous proclamation and explanation of his fifty names. If the creation of
the universe were the prime purpose of the epic, much more emphasis should have been placed on this point.

As it is, there can be no doubt that, in its present form,
Enûma elish is first and foremost a literary monument in honor
of Marduk as the champion of the gods and the creator of heav-
en and earth. Its prime object is to offer cosmological reasons
for Marduk's advancement from the position as chief god of
Babylon to that of head of the entire Babylonian pantheon.
This was achieved by attributing to him the defeat of Tiʾâmat
and the creation and maintenance of the universe. The description of the birth of the gods and of the subsequent struggle between Ea and Apsû and the account of the origin of the universe
were added mainly for the purpose of furthering the cause of
Marduk; the former was included as the antecedent to Marduk's conflict with Tiʾâmat and his accession to supreme power
among the gods, while the latter, the story of the creation of the
universe, was added not so much for the sake of giving an account of how all things came into being, but chiefly because it
further served to enhance the glory of Marduk and helped to
justify his claim to sovereignty over all things visible and in-
visible.

Next to the purpose of singing the praises of Marduk comes
the desire, on the part of the Babylonian priests, who were responsible for the composition of this epic, to sing the praises of
Babylon, the city of Marduk, and to strengthen her claim to
supremacy over all the cities of the land. Babylon's claim to
supremacy was justified already by the fact that it was Babylon's god who had conquered Tiʾâmat and had created and organized the universe. It was further supported by tracing
Babylon's origin back to the very beginnings of time and by
attributing her foundation to the great Anunnaki themselves,
who built Babylon as a dwelling place for Marduk and the gods
in general (Tablet VI:45–73). Our epic is thus not only a religious treatise but also a political one.

THE SOURCES OF THE EPIC

It is generally admitted that *Enûma elish*, though it is one of the literary masterpieces of the Babylonian Semites, is undoubtedly based on the cosmology of the Sumerians and that the central figure of the Sumerian story was Enlil, the most important god in Babylonia until Marduk's rise to supremacy. For not only do all the gods, with the exception of Tiᵃâmat, appear to have Sumerian names but some of the gods themselves, such as Apsû, Anu, and Enlil, are admittedly Sumerian. Moreover, the majority of the monsters which Tiᵃâmat bore (Tablet I:132–42) and almost all the winds created by Marduk (Tablet IV:45–46) likewise have Sumerian names. Even man himself is called by a Sumerian term, *lullû*, which is immediately translated by the Semitic *amêlu* (Tablet VI:6–7).[3] Furthermore, the separation of the primeval world matter into heaven and earth is a feat which the Sumerians ascribed to Enlil, the personified air, for it is the atmosphere which, placed between the sky and the earth, holds them apart.[4] Another important point to be considered in this connection is the fact that the Semites in Babylonia became in general the heirs of the Sumerians, and as such they took over, with certain modifications, their script and literature, their religion, their culture and civilization. But how much of *Enûma elish* must be traced to Sumerian sources cannot be ascertained with any degree of finality until Sumerian cosmology is better known as to both content and origin, for, as S. N. Kramer has remarked,[5] it is quite possible that there are "traces of Semitic influence in even the earliest known Sumerian mythology just as we find them in case of the Sumerian language."[6]

[3] It has been asserted that the explanations of Marduk's names in Tablet VII are derived throughout from a Sumerian original. But the assertion cannot be proved (see A. Ungnad's article in *Zeitschrift für Assyriologie*, XXXI [1917/18], 153–55).

[4] Cf. S. N. Kramer in the *Journal of the American Oriental Society*, LXIII (1943), 72, 2, and Jacobsen in *The Intellectual Adventure. . . .* , pp. 169 and 178.

[5] In the *Journal of the American Oriental Society*, LXIII, 71, n. 4.

[6] On the Sumerian creation materials see Kramer's remarks *ibid.*, pp. 70–73, his book *Sumerian Mythology* (Philadelphia, 1944), and Jacobsen's review of the latter in the *Journal of Near Eastern Studies*, V (1946), 128–52.

THE DATE OF COMPOSITION

When our poem was composed in approximately its present Semitic form we cannot as yet determine with certainty. The tablets and fragments from Ashurbanipal's library at Nineveh belong to the seventh century B.C.; those from the city of Ashur date back to approximately 1000 B.C.; while those from Kish, the fragment from Uruk, and those of uncertain provenance belong to the sixth century B.C. and later. But all these tablets are copies of older ones, as indicated by the colophons at the ends of the different tablets and by the fact that on the tablets from Ashur the scribes usually retained the name of Marduk, instead of substituting for it that of the god of Ashur, which shows that they copied from Babylonian originals. The date for the composition of our epic must therefore be pushed back beyond the date of the oldest copies at our disposal, and that will bring it somewhere beyond 1000 B.C.

However, we have reason to push it back much further. The inscription of Agum II (fifteenth century B.C.), the ninth king of the Kassite Dynasty, following almost immediately upon the First Babylonian Dynasty, seems to show that *Enûma elish* existed already during the fifteenth century B.C. In this inscription Agum records the restoration of the statues of Marduk and his consort Ṣarpanîtu, which had been carried away to the land Ḫanî, and describes the works of art with which he embellished the statues and sanctuaries of these two divinities. He states, among other things, that on the panels of the doors of the holy chambers he had his craftsmen represent a number of monsters. He mentions the viper, the *laḫmu*, the bison, the great lion, the mad dog, the dragonfly, and the goat-fish. These monsters, with the exception of the goat-fish, are identical with those which Marduk vanquished in his combat with Tiʾâmat (Tablet I:140–43). This similarity alone, of course, proves nothing as to the date of *Enûma elish*, because one could easily argue that the monsters in question formed part of general Babylonian mythology and that both passages reverted to the same fountain-head. But their association with Marduk seems to reveal the in-

14 THE BABYLONIAN GENESIS

fluence of *Enûma eliš* and, consequently, seems to indicate that our epic was composed at least before the end of Agum's reign.[7]

But we have better reasons than this for assuming an even earlier date. For if we consider that the two main objects of the epic are to justify Marduk's ascendancy to supreme rulership over all the Babylonian divinities and to support Babylon's claim to pre-eminence above all the other cities in the country, as we have seen, and that Babylon rose to political supremacy during the First Babylonian Dynasty (1894–1595),[8] particularly under the energetic king Hammurabi (1792–1750), and that during this dynasty Marduk became the national god,[9] it would seem that the poem, in approximately its present form, was composed some time during the First Babylonian Dynasty. The language of the epic points in the same direction, as observed by W. von Soden.[10]

[7] Cf. S. Langdon, *The Babylonian Epic of Creation* (Oxford, 1923), pp. 10–11. If I. J. Gelb's contention, in the *Journal of Near Eastern Studies*, VIII (1949), 348, n. 12, that the Agum inscription is a forgery proves correct, the argument based on this document of course falls to the ground.

[8] The dates which are here provisionally accepted are those of Sidney Smith, *Alalakh and Chronology* (London, 1940), p. 29.

[9] The real beginning of Marduk's advancement dates to the reign of Hammurabi. Cf. the opening lines of the prologue to the Code of Hammurabi: "When the exalted Anu, the king of the Anunnaki, (and) Enlil, the lord of heaven and earth, who determine the destinies of the land, committed the sovereignty over all the people to Marduk, the first-born son of Ea; (when) they made him great among the Igigi; (when) they proclaimed to Babylon his exalted name; (when) they made it unsurpassable in the regions of the world (and) in its midst established for him an everlasting kingdom whose foundations are firm as heaven and earth: at that time Anu and Enlil called me, Hammurabi, the reverent prince, the worshipper of the gods, by my name, to cause justice to prevail in the land, to destroy the wicked and the evil, to prevent the strong from oppressing the weak, to go forth like the sun over the human race, to enlighten the land and to further the welfare of the people" (R. F. Harper, *The Code of Ḫammurabi, King of Babylon* [Chicago and London, 1904]); Bruno Meissner, *Babylonien und Assyrien*, II (Heidelberg, 1925), 46; and O. E. Ravn in *Acta orientalia*, VII (1929), 81–90.

[10] In his study on the hymnic-epical dialect of Akkadian, published in *Zeitschrift für Assyriologie*, XL (1931), 163–227, and XLI (1933), 90–183. See esp. *ibid.*, XLI, 177–81.

THE METER OF THE POEM

Our epic was intended for recitation. Hence it was cast into poetry, since this is the most appealing and most effective method of expression for that purpose. Babylonian poetry, like Hebrew, has no rhyme, but it has rhythm, or meter. In accordance with the rules of Babylonian poetry, the lines fall into distichs, or couplets, as we can see, for example, from the fact that, where space permits it, the two verses forming a couplet are frequently written on the same line, separated by two small dividing wedges. The second line of a distich usually forms a contrast, a parallel, or a supplement to the first, as exemplified by the following lines of the creation story:

Tablet I:1-2:   When above the heaven had not (yet) been named,
          (And) below the earth had not (yet) been called by a name;
Tablet I:25-26: Apsû could not diminish their clamor,
          And Tiᵃmat was silent in regard to their [behavior];
Tablet I:33-34: They went and reposed before Tiᵃmat;
          They took counsel concerning the gods, their first-born.

Quite frequently two distichs unite to form a quatrain, or a stanza of four lines. Compare, for example, Tablet I:37-40:

          Their way has become painful to me,
          By day I cannot rest, by night I cannot sleep;
          I will destroy (them) and put an end to their way,
          That silence be established, and then let us sleep!

In our epic, each of the two lines, or verses, of a distich falls into halves, divided by a well-marked caesura, and each half of a line may again be divided into two parts, each of which contains, as a rule, a single accented word or phrase. In *Enûma elish*, as Benno Landsberger pointed out in a meeting of the Assyrian Dictionary staff, the final accent of a line usually rests on the second-last syllable, hardly ever on the last or the third-last syllable (on the last syllable are accented, e.g., Tablet IV: 19 and 49; on the third-last syllable, e.g., Tablets I:42 and 48; II:4 and 107; and III:58).

That this fourfold division of each line actually exists is clear from the tablet Sp. II. 265a[11]—which, however, has nothing to

[11] Published by Heinrich Zimmern in *Zeitschrift für Assyriologie*, X (1895), 17–18, and republished by J. A. Craig, *Assyrian and Babylonian Religious Texts*, I (Leipzig, 1895), 44–45.

do with the creation story—on which the scribe has drawn a vertical line not only after the half-verses but also after each quarter-verse. Some of the scribes who copied *Enûma elish* left a space between the halves of each line and so divided each verse into two main parts, thus indicating at least the caesura in the middle of each verse. This fourfold division of each line, together with its four accents, can well be illustrated by the first two verses of our poem:

| enûma | élish | lâ nabû | shamâmu |
| sháplish | ámmatum | shúma | lâ zákrat[12] |

"ENÛMA ELISH" AND THE NEW YEAR'S FESTIVAL

At the end of the fourth day of the New Year's celebration in Babylon, which lasted from the first to the eleventh of Nisan, *Enûma elish* was recited in its entirety by the high priest before the statue of Marduk.[13] Then in the course of the festival, on an undetermined day, *Enûma elish* was again recited, or chanted. Parts of the epic may even have been dramatized, the king and the priests playing the roles of Marduk, Ti'âmat, Kingu, and other figures in the story.

The reason for the second recitation of the epic is expressly stated in *Keilschrifttexte aus Assur religiösen Inhalts*, Nos. 143: 34 and 219:8: "*Enûma elish* which is recited before Bêl,which they chant in the month of Nisan, (it is) because he is held prisoner." The chanting of the epic is here apparently intended as a magical aid in Marduk's deliverance from imprisonment, the precise nature of which is not clear.[14]

The reason for the first recitation, on the fourth of Nisan, is not given in any of the available cuneiform sources. We are therefore dependent on conjecture.

[12] For more information on the meter in Babylonian poetry and for further references see Friedrich Delitzsch, *Das Babylonische Weltschöpfungsepos* (Leipzig, 1896), pp. 60–68; L. W. King, *The Seven Tablets of Creation*, I, cxxii f.; Meissner, *op. cit.*, II, 152–55; and E. Sievers in *Zeitschrift für Assyriologie*, XXXVIII (1929), 1–38.

[13] F. Thureau-Dangin, *Rituels accadiens* (Paris, 1921), p. 136: 279–84.

[14] On the question of Marduk's death and resurrection see P. Jensen in *Orientalistische Literaturzeitung*, Vol. XXVII (1924), cols. 573–77, and Zimmern in *Der alte Orient*, XXV, 3 (1926), 14–16.

S. A. Pallis[15] has suggested that the recital was for the purpose of exorcising all that is evil, just as the Babylonian creation myth "When Anu had created the heavens" was recited to keep away the evil influence of the demons during and after the restoration of the temple, by proclaiming the might and power of the gods (see p. 65 of this book). However, the proper time for a recital with this object in view would have been the first day of the festival, and it is unlikely that this ceremony was performed twice for the same purpose.

It is possible that on this occasion the epic was recited as a magic formula against the coming inundation of Babylonia caused by the rise of the Tigris and the Euphrates following the melting of the snows in the mountains of Armenia and Kurdistan; for at the time of these floods it seemed as if the primordial chaotic condition of "water, water everywhere" were to return. This possibility is suggested by Tablet VII: 132–34: "May he subdue Tiʾâmat, may he distress her life, and may it be short! Until future (generations of) men, when the (present) days have grown old, may she retreat without hindrance, may she withdraw forever!" The recitation of *Enûma elish* presumably reflects the annual battle between Marduk and the watery chaos produced by the spring inundations.

On the other hand, it is also possible that the recitation and the supposed partial dramatization of *Enûma elish* were in honor of Marduk. For this was the festival of Marduk, the creator of the present world order; it was the season when the various gods of the land came to Babylon "to take the hands" of Marduk.[16] At the same time it was probably the hope of the Babylonians that this manifestation of their devotion to the king of the gods would assure a more favorable destiny for their country, especially considering that it was during this festival, on the eighth and the ninth of Nisan, that the destinies of the land were determined for the ensuing year.[17]

[15] *The Babylonian Akîtu Festival* (Copenhagen, 1926), pp. 298 and 212.

[16] See T. G. Pinches in the *Proceedings of the Society of Biblical Archaeology*, XXX (1908), 80 (cf. also Zimmern in *Der alte Orient*, XXV, No. 3, 14).

[17] Sir H. C. Rawlinson, *The Cuneiform Inscriptions of Western Asia*, Vol. I (London, 1861), Pl. 54, col. ii, 54–65; translated by S. Langdon, *Die Neubabylonischen Königsinschriften* (Leipzig, 1912), p. 126.

TABLET I

1. When above the heaven had not (yet) been named,[18]
2. (And) below the earth had not (yet) been called by a name;[18]
3. (When) Apsû primeval, their begetter,[19]
4. Mummu,[20] (and) Tiᵓâmat, she who gave birth to them all,
5. (Still) mingled their waters together,
6. And no pasture land had been formed (and) not (even) a reed marsh was to be seen;
7. When none of the (other) gods had been brought into being,
8. (When) they had not (yet) been called by (their) name(s, and their) destinies had not (yet) been fixed,
9. (At that time) were the gods created within them.[21]
10. Laḫmu and Laḫâmu came into being; they were called by (their) names.[22]
11. Even before they had grown up (and) become tall,
12. Anshar and Kishar were created; they surpassed them (in stature).
13. They lived many days, adding years (to days).
14. Anu was their heir presumptive, the rival of his fathers;
15. Yea, Anu, his first-born, equaled Anshar.[23]
16. And Anu begot Nudimmud,[24] his likeness.
17. Nudimmud, the master of his fathers was he;[25]
18. He was broad of understanding, wise, mighty in strength,
19. Much stronger than his grandfather, Anshar;
20. He had no rival among the gods his brothers.[26]

[18] I.e., did not yet exist as such.

[19] I.e., the begetter of the gods.

[20] On Mummu see the writer's article in the *Journal of Near Eastern Studies*, VII (1948), 98–105.

[21] Within Apsû and Tiᵓâmat.

[22] This line shows that forms or beings can exist before they have been named.

[23] Cf. Jensen in *Orientalistische Literaturzeitung*, Vol. XXVIII (1925), col. 22.

[24] Another name for Ea.

[25] In the sense that his fathers were subject to his will, because of his great wisdom and his control over magic (Anton Deimel, *"Enuma Eliš" und Hexaëmeron* [Rome, 1934], p. 30).

[26] A variant has "fathers."

TABLET I—*Continued*

21. The divine brothers gathered together.
22. They disturbed Tiʾâmat and assaulted(?) their keeper;[27]
23. Yea, they disturbed the inner parts of Tiʾâmat,
24. Moving (and) running about[27a] in the divine abode(?).
25. Apsû could not diminish their clamor,
26. And Tiʾâmat was silent in regard to their [behavior].
27. Yet, their doing was painful [to them].
28. Their way was not good. . . . .
29. Then Apsû, the begetter of the great gods,
30. Called Mummu, his vizier, and said to him:
31. "Mummu, my vizier, who gladdenest my heart,
32. Come, let us [go] to Tiʾâmat!"
33. They went and reposed before Tiʾâmat;
34. They took counsel about the matter concerning the gods, their first-born.
35. Apsû opened his mouth
36. And said to Tiʾâmat in a loud voice:
37. "Their way has become painful to me,
38. By day I cannot rest, by night I cannot sleep;
39. I will destroy (them) and put an end to their way,
40. That silence be established, and then let us sleep!"
41. When Tiʾâmat heard this,
42. She was wroth and cried out to her husband;
43. She cried out and raged furiously, she alone.
44. She pondered the evil in her heart (and said):
45. "Why should we destroy that which we ourselves have brought forth?
46. Their way is indeed very painful, but let us take it good-naturedly!"
47. Mummu spoke up and counseled Apsû;
48. [. . . .] and unfavorable was the advice of his Mummu:
49. "Yes, my father, destroy (their) disorderly way;
50. (Then) verily thou shalt have rest by day (and) sleep by night!"

[27] I.e., Apsû. For the phrase "their keeper" cf. Ps. 121:4, which has "the keeper of Israel."

[27a] Reading *i-na-shu iʾ-a-ru* with A. Poebel.

TABLET I—*Continued*

51. When Apsû [hear]d it, his face grew bright,
52. Because of the evil he planned against the gods his children.
53. Mummu embraced [his] neck,
54. Sat down on his knee, and kissed him.
55. Whatever they planned in their assembly
56. Was communicated to the gods, their first-born.
57. When the gods heard (it), they hasten(ed) about;
58. They took to silence, they sat quietly.
59. The one of supreme understanding, the skilful (and) wise,
60. Ea, who understands everything, saw through their plan.[28]
61. He made and established against it a magical circle for all.
62. He skilfully composed his overpowering, holy incantation.
63. He recited it and thus caused (it) to be upon the water.[29]
64. He poured out sleep upon him, (so that) he slept soundly.[30]
65. When he had put Apsû to sleep, (Apsû) being suffused with sleep,
66. Mummu, his adviser,[31] . . . . .
67. He loosened his band (and) tore off [his] tiara;
68. He carried off his splendor[32] (and) put (it) on himself.[33]
69. When he had (thus) subdued Apsû, he slew him.
70. Mummu he shut in (and) barred (the door) against him.
71. On Apsû he established his dwelling place;

[28] The plan of Apsû and Mummu. Ea realized its full consequences and knew how it could be foiled.

[29] I.e., the sweet-water Apsû.

[30] Reading, with Ebeling, *ṭu-ub shit-tum*, instead of *ṭu-ub-qit-tum* ("a cavern"), which does not give any sense.

[31] Reading *tam-la-ku*, with A. Poebel. In a synonym list published by W. von Soden, *Die lexikalischen Tafelserien der Babylonier und Assyrer in den Berliner Museen* (Berlin, 1933), No. 2, col. iii, l. 162, *tam-la-ku* is equated with *mil-ku*, "advice," "adviser." Analogous formations are *tamkâru*, "merchant"; *têniqu*, "suckling"; *tarbû*, "novice"; *tênû*, "successor"; *targigu*, "scoundrel"; *tashlishu*, "the third on the chariot"; etc.

[32] In this and the preceding line the possessive pronominal form "his" refers to Apsû, not to Mummu, who was only the vizier and as such was not entitled to wear a crown or a tiara.

[33] *Var.*: (and) he, Ea, p[ut (it) on him]self. With this line cf. Ps. 104:2.

TABLET I—*Continued*

72. Mummu he seized for himself, holding (him) by his nose-rope.
73. After Ea had vanquished (and) subdued his enemies,
74. Had established his victory over his foes,
75. (And) had peacefully rested in his abode,
76. He named it *Apsû* and appointed (it) for shrines.
77. In his place he founded his chamber;
78. (There) Ea (and) Damkina, his wife, dwelt in splendor.
79. In the chamber of fates, the abode of destinies,
80. The wisest of the wise, the wisest of the gods, *the* god was begotten.
81. Within the *Apsû* Marduk was born;
82. Within the holy *Apsû* [Marduk] was born.
83. He who begot him was Ea, his father;
84. Damki[na], his mother, was she who bore him.
85. He sucked[34] the breasts of goddesses.
86. The nurse that cared for him filled (him) with awe-inspiring majesty.
87. Enticing was his figure, flashing the look of his eyes,
88. Manly was his going-forth, a leader(?)[35] from the beginning.
89. When E[a], his father that begot (him), saw him,
90. He rejoiced, he beamed, his heart was filled with joy.
91. He distinguished(?) him and con[ferred upon him(?)] dou[ble] equality with the gods,
92. (So that) he was highly exalted (and) surpassed them in everything.
93. Artfully arranged beyond comprehension were his members,
94. Not fit for (human) understanding, hard to look upon.
95. Four were his eyes, four were his ears.

[34] *Var.*: she caused him to suck.

[35] Tentatively taking *mu-shìr* to stand for *mushshir*, which occurs in Ludwig Abel and Hugo Winckler, *Keilschrifttexte zum Gebrauch bei Vorlesungen* (Berlin, 1890), p. 60:24. The context favors a meaning such as "leader"; for what the gods needed in their impending struggle, to which this passage leads up, was a vigorous leader in battle. Marduk by his very appearance and demeanor gave promise of being just such a figure, looking like a "born leader."

TABLET I—*Continued*

96. When his lips moved, fire blazed forth.
97. Each of (his) four ears grew large,
98. And likewise (his) eyes, to see everything.
99. He was exalted among the gods, surpassing was [his] form;
100. His members were gigantic, he was surpassing in height.
101. Mâriyûtu, Mâriyûtu:
102. Son of the sun-god, the sun-god of the go[ds]![36]
103. He was clothed with the rays of ten gods, exceedingly powerful was he;
104. The te[rror-inspiring ma]jesty with its consuming brightness(?) rested upon him.
105. [. . . .] the four winds did Anu create,
106. To restrain with his [. . . .] the strong(est) of the host.[37]
107. He caused waves and disturbed Ti'âmat.
108. Disturbed is Ti'âmat, and day and night she (restlessly) hastens about.
109. ꜔The gods꜕ were not at rest, carrying on(?) like the storm(?);
110. They planned evil in their heart(s).
111. They said to Ti'âmat, their mother:[37a]
112. "When they slew Apsû, thy spouse,
113. Thou didst not march at his side, but thou didst sit quietly.[38]
114. He made . . . . fear.

[36] With the translation of this line cf. Poebel's article in the *American Journal of Semitic Languages and Literatures*, LI (1934/35), 172. Line 101 contains a name of Marduk, while l. 102 offers an analysis and interpretation of the same after the method employed in Tablets VI and VII. We probably have here an exclamation by the poet or poets, which leads over to the following lines. There is no evidence that "the older deities greeted the new-born god Marduk" with this name (as against J. Lewy in *Orientalia*, XV [New ser., 1946], 380). Marduk appears in this passage not as a "new-born god" but as a full-grown god, as shown by the immediately preceding lines.

[37] I.e., the host of monsters whose birth is recorded in ll. 132–45 (cf. Tablet IV:115–16). This and the preceding line are doubtless anticipatory, like the description of the might of Marduk.

[37a] According to the photo.

[38] Ti'âmat took no part in Apsû and Mummu's struggle against the gods. And when she did engage in active hostilities, it was only to avenge Apsû, at the instigation of some of the gods, of whom Kingu was the ringleader (cf. Tablet VI: 29 f.), for which reason Ti'âmat placed him in command of her forces.

TABLET I—*Continued*

115. Disturbed is thine interior, and we cannot rest.

116. Remember(?) Apsû, thy spouse,

117. And Mummu, who were vanquished; thou dwellest alone.[39]

118. Thou art [not a m[other], rest[less]ly thou runnest about.

119. [. . . .] thou dost not love us (anymore).

120. [. . . .] . . . ., our eyes are heavy.

121. [. . . .] without ceasing(?) let us sleep!

122. [Go to batt]le(?) (and) requite them!

123. [. . . .] and give (them) over to the storm!"

124. [When] Tiʾâmat [heard it], the word pleased her,[40]

125. [And she said: ". . . .] . . . . let us make storm.

126. [. . . .] and the gods in the midst of [. . . .].

127. [. . . . let us] make war, against the gods let us [. . . .]!"

128. They [separated themselves(?)] and went to the side of Tiʾâmat;

129. They [were angry], they plotted, not resting day or [night];

130. They [took up] the fight, fuming (and) raging;

131. They held a meeting and planned the conflict.

132. Mother Hubur,[41] who fashions all things,

133. Added (thereto) irresistible weapons, bearing monster serpents

134. [Sharp] of tooth (and) not sparing the fang(?).

135. [With poison] instead of blood she filled [their] bodies.

136. Ferocious [dra]gons she cl[othed] with terror,

137. She crowned (them) with fear-inspiring glory (and) made (them) like gods,

138. So that he who would look upon them should pe[rish] from terror,

139. So that their bodies might leap forward and none turn back [their breasts].

140. She set up the viper, the dragon, and the *laḫâmu*,[42]

[39] *Var.*: Dost thou not dwell alone? [40] Reading *i-ṭib el-sha*.

[41] Another designation for Tiʾâmat, as is evident from a comparison of l. 154 with Tablet IV:65–66 and 81. In the first passage Mother Hubur calls Kingu her spouse, while in the last two passages Kingu is spoken of as the spouse of Tiʾâmat.

[42] Here *laḫâmu* is some kind of monster and has nothing to do with the goddess Laḫâmu mentioned at the beginning of this tablet.

TABLET I—*Continued*

141. The great lion,[43] the mad dog,[43] and the scorpion-man,
142. Driving storm demons, the dragonfly, and the bis[on],[44]
143. Bearing unsparing weapons, unafraid of ba[ttle].
144. Powerful were her decrees, irresistible were they.
145. Altogether(?) eleven (kinds of monsters) of this sort she brought [into being].
146. Of those among the gods, her[45] first-born, who formed her [assembly],
147. She exalted Kingu; in their midst she made him great.
148. To march at the head of the army, to direct the for[ces],
149. To raise the weapons for the engagement, to launch the attack,
150. The high command of the battle,
151. She intrusted to his hand; she caused him to sit in the assembly, (saying:)
152. "I have cast the spell for thee, I have made thee great in the assembly of the gods.
153. The dominion over all the gods I have given into thy hand.
154. Mayest thou be highly exalted, thou, my unique spouse!
155. May thy names become greater than (those of) all the Anunnaki!"
156. She gave him the tablet of destinies, she fastened (it) upon his breast, (saying:)
157. "As for thee, thy command shall not be changed, [the word of thy mouth] shall be dependable!"
158. Now when Kingu had been exalted (and) had received [supreme dominion],
159. [They[46] decreed] the destinies to the gods, her sons,[47] (saying:)
160. "May the opening of your mouths [quiet] the fire-god![48]

[43] A variant has the plural.

[44] For the translation of the two last terms see B. Landsberger, *Die Fauna des alten Mesopotamien* (Leipzig, 1934), pp. 123 and 93.

[45] *Var.*: their first-born (i.e., Apsû and Tiʾâmat's).

[46] Kingu and Tiʾâmat (cf. Tablet II:46).

[47] The gods who had gone over to the side of Tiʾâmat (cf. also Tablet III:50 and 108).

[48] Probably Marduk (cf. Tablets I:96 and IV:39–40).

TABLET I—*Continued*

161. May thy overpowering poison vanquish the (opposing) might!"[49]

CATCH LINE

After Tiâmat had made strong [preparations].

COLOPHON I

1. First tablet of *Enûma elish;* [written] like [its] original [and collated].
2. The tablet of Nabû-balâṭsu-iqbî, the son of Naid-Ma[rduk].
3. By the hand of Nabû-balâṭsu-iqbî, the son of ⸢Naid-Marduk . . . .⸣.

COLOPHON II

1. First tablet of *Enûma elish,* after the ta[blet . . . .],
2. A copy from Babylon; written like its original [and collated].
3. The tablet of Nabû-mushêtiq-ûmi, the son of [. . . .].
4. He who fears Marduk and Ṣarpanî[tu shall not take it away illegitimately]
5. Or withhold (it) from use ⸢. . . .⸣.
6. The month of Iyyar, the ninth day, the twenty-seventh year of D[arius].

TABLET II

1. After Tiâmat had made str[ong] preparations,
2. She made ready to join battle with the gods her offspring.
3. ⸢To avenge⸣ Apsû, Tiâmat did (this) evil.
4. How she got ready for the attack was revealed to Ea.
5. When Ea heard of this matter,
6. He became benumbed with f[ea]r and sat in silent gloom.
7. Af[ter he had] reflected on (the matter) and his wrath had subsided,
8. He went to Anshar, his (grand)father.
9. And when he had [co]me into the presence of Anshar, his grandfather,
10. He communicated to him all that Tiâmat had planned.

[49] The translation of this line is provisional.

TABLET II—*Continued*

11. "My father, Ti᾽âmat, our bearer, hates us.
12. She held a meeting and raged furiously.
13. All the gods went over to her;
14. Even those whom ye have created march at her side.
15. They separated themselves(?) and went over to the side of Ti᾽âmat;
16. They were angry, they plotted, not resting day or night;
17. They took up the fight, fuming and raging;
18. They held a meeting and planned the conflict.
19. Mother Ḫubur, who fashions all things,
20. Added (thereto) irresistible weapons, bearing monster serpents
21. Sharp of tooth and not sparing the fang(?).
22. With poison instead of blood she filled their bodies.
23. Ferocious dragons she clothed with terror,
24. She crowned them with fear-inspiring glory (and) made them like gods,
25. So that he who would look upon them should perish from terror,
26. So that their bodies might leap forward and none turn back their breasts.
27. She set up the viper, the dragon,[50] and the *laḫâmu*,
28. The great lion, the mad dog, and the scorpion-man,
29. Driving storm demons, the dragonfly, and the bison,
30. Bearing unsparing weapons, unafraid of battle.
31. Powerful are her decrees, irresistible are they.
32. Altogether(?) eleven (kinds of monsters) of this sort she brought into being.
33. Of those among the gods, her first-born, who formed her assembly,
34. She exalted Kingu; in their midst she made him great.
35. To march at the head of the army, to direct the forces,
36. To raise the weapons for the engagement, to launch the attack,
37. The high command of the battle,

[50] A variant has "dragons."

TABLET II—*Continued*

38. [She int]rusted to his hand; she caused him to sit in the assembly, (saying:)
39. '[I have] cast the spell for thee, I have made thee great in the assembly of the gods.
40. The dominion over all the gods I have given [into thy h]and.
41. Mayest thou be highly exalted, thou, my unique spouse!
42. [May] thy names become greater than (those of) [the Anun]naki!'
43. [She ga]ve him the tablet of destinies, she fa[sten]ed (it) upon his breast, (saying:)
44. '[As for thee], thy command shall not be changed, the word of thy mouth shall be dependable!'
45. Now when Kingu had been exalted (and) had received supreme dominion,
46. They decreed the destinies of [the gods], her sons, (saying:)
47. 'May [the opening] of your months quiet the fire-god!
48. May [thy overpowering poison] vanquish the (opposing) might!' "
49. [When Anshar heard that Tiᵖâma]t was stirred profoundly,
50. [He smote his thigh and] bit his lip.[51]
51. [His heart was full of gloom], his body did not rest.
52. [. . . .] he suppresses his groaning.
53. [He says to Ea: "Arise, my son, go to] battle!
54. [The weapon which thou ha]st made thou shalt bear.
55. Thou hast slain Apsû [. . . .];
56. [Slay thou also(?) Kin]gu, who goes before her.
57. [. . . .] wisdom."
58. Nudi[mmud, the counselor of the gods, answered him, (saying:)]
59–70. (*Destroyed. The break no doubt recorded Nudimmud's, i.e., Ea's, failure,*[52] *even though he had succeeded in defeating Apsû. Anshar then turns to his son Anu.*)
71. [. . . . Anshar cr]ied out [. . . .] in anger(?);
72. [To Anu], his son, he spoke [a word], (saying:)
73. "[My first-born], thou there! my mighty hero,

[51] Signs of grief or anger.   [52] Cf. Tablet III:54.

TABLET II—*Continued*

74. Whose [po]wer is [great], whose onslaught is irresistible,
75. [Go a]nd stand thou before Tiᵖâmat,
76. [That] her spirit [become quiet and] her heart calm down.
77. [If] she does not hearken to thy word,
78. Speak our [word(?)] to her, that she may be quieted."
79. [When he had heard] the words of his father, Anshar,
80. [He took a direct rou]te to her and pursued the way to her.
81. Anu [drew nigh], but perceiving the (strategic) plan of Tiᵖâmat
82. And [not being able to withstand her], he turned back.⁵³
83. [He went in terror to] his [father], Anshar.
84. [Concerning Tiᵖâmat thus he] spoke to him:
85. "[. . .] . of her hand is . . . . upon me!"
86. Anshar lapsed into silence, looking upon the ground.
87. He shakes his locks,⁵⁴ shaking his head at Ea.
88. All the Anunnaki were assembled at the place.
89. Their lips were closed, [they sat in] silence.
90. "No god whatever can go t[o battle]
91. (And) escape w[ith his life] from the presence of Tiᵖâmat."
92. Lord Anshar, the father of the gods, [arose in] majesty;
93. His heart [prom]pted (him) [to speak to the Anunnaki]:
94. "[He] whose [strength] is mighty shall be the avenger of [his] father.
95. [That one is] the . . . . in battle, the valia[nt] Mar[duk]!"
96. Ea called [Marduk] to [his] private room;
97. [He ad]vised⁵⁵ (him), telling him the plan⁵⁶ of his heart:
98. "Marduk, consider my idea, hearken to thy father.
99. Thou art he, my son, who relieves his heart;
100. Draw nigh [into the presence of] Anshar, (ready) for battle(?);
101. [Speak and] stand forth; when he sees thee, he will be at rest."

⁵³ Cf. Tablet III:53.

⁵⁴ See Landsberger *apud* Thureau-Dangin in *Syria*, XII (1931), 234, "L. 12."

⁵⁵ Reading [*im*]-*li-ka*.

⁵⁶ In this passage *ma-ak* is probably the apocopated construct of *makû*. The term seems to be used as a synonym of *ṭêmu*, occurring in the next line.

TABLET II—*Continued*

102. The lord[57] was glad at the word of his father;
103. He drew nigh and stood before Anshar.
104. When Anshar saw him, his heart was filled with joy;
105. He kissed his lips, his fear was removed.
106. "[Anshar], be not silent, (but) open thy lips;[58]
107. I will go and accomplish all that is in thy heart!
108. [Yea, Anshar], be not silent, (but) open thy lips;
109. [I will g]o and accomplish all that is in thy heart!
110. What man is it who has brought battle against thee?
111. [. . . . T]iʾâmat, who is a woman, is coming against thee with arms!
112. [My father, c]reator, be glad and rejoice;
113. Soon thou shalt trample upon the neck of Tiʾâmat!
114. [Yea, my father, c]reator, be glad and rejoice;
115. Soon thou shalt trample upon [the neck of] Tiʾâmat!"
116. "My [so]n, who knowest all wisdom,
117. Quiet [Tiʾâmat] with thy holy incantation.
118. On the storm [chari]ot(?) quickly pursue (the way)!
119. [. . . .] . . . . turn (her) back!"
120. The lord [was glad] at the word of his father;
121. His heart [ex]ulted, and he said to his father:
122. "Lord of the gods, destiny of the great gods,[59]
123. If I am indeed to be your avenger,
124. To vanquish Tiʾâmat and to keep you alive,
125. Convene the assembly and proclaim my lot supreme.
126. When ye are joyfully seated together in the Court of Assembly,
127. May I through the utterance of my mouth determine the destinies, instead of[60] you.

[57] Marduk.

[58] See Delitzsch's posthumous article in *Archiv für Orientforschung*, VI (1930/31), 223.

[59] I.e., the one who determines the destinies of the great gods.

[60] Cf. Delitzsch, *Das babylonische Weltschöpfungsepos*, pp. 134 f. In view of the next two lines and of Tablet IV:4-29, where Marduk's destiny is made "supreme among the gods" and Marduk is given "kingship over the totality of the whole universe," there can hardly be any doubt that *kîma* here has the meaning "instead of." Marduk demands supreme and undisputed authority as the price for

TABLET II—*Continued*

128. Whatever I create shall remain unaltered,
129. The command of my lips shall not return (void), it shall not be changed."

CATCH LINE

Anshar opened his mouth

COLOPHON I

1. Second [tablet of] *Enûma elish;* [written] according to [the tablet]
2. [. . . .], a copy from Ashur.
3. [. . . . .].

COLOPHON II

1. Written [like] its [original] and collated. The tablet of Nabû-aḫḫê-iddina,
2. [The son of] Eṭir-bêl, the son of a priest of the god Mash.[61] One shall not withhold (it) from use.

TABLET III

1. Anshar opened his mouth
2. And addressed (these) words to Kaka, his vizier:
3. "Kaka, my vizier, who gladdenest my heart,
4. Unto Laḫmu (and) Laḫâmu I will send thee;
5. Thou knowest (how) to [disce]rn (and) art able to relate.
6. Cause the gods my fathers to be brought before me.
7. [Let] them bring all the gods to me!
8. Let them converse (and) sit down to a banquet.
9. Let them eat bread (and) prepare wine.[62]

---

risking his life in combat with Tiᵓâmat. When therefore the gods, at the New Year's festival, convened in the Court of Assembly, "they reverently waited" on Marduk, the "king of the gods of heaven and earth," and in that spirit they decided the destinies. The gods, indeed, "continue to 'determine destinies' long after Marduk has received the powers he here desires" (Jacobsen in the *Journal of Near Eastern Studies,* II [1943], 170, n. 62); but the final decision rested with Marduk, so that in the last analysis it was he who decided the fates.

[61] Another name for the warrior-god Ninurta.

[62] The reference is probably to the preparation of wine for immediate use and greater enjoyment. The passage probably alludes to the widespread custom of

TABLET III—*Continued*

10. For [Marduk], their avenger, let them decree the destiny.
11. Set out, O Kaka, go, and stand thou before them.
12. What I am about to tell thee repeat unto them:
13. 'Anshar, your son, has sent me.
14. [The command of] his heart he has charged me to convey,
15. [Saying: "Tiʾâ]mat, our bearer, hates us.
16. She heʾ[ld a meeting] and raged furiously.
17. All the gods went over to her;
18. Even those whom ye have created march at her side.
19. They separated themselves(?) and went over to the side of Tiʾâmat;
20. They were angry, they plotted, not resting day or night;
21. They took up the fight, fuming and raging;
22. They held a meeting and planned the conflict.
23. Mother Ḫubur, who fashions all things,
24. Added (thereto) irresistible weapons, bearing monster serpents
25. Sharp of tooth and not sparing the fang(?).
26. With poison instead of blood she filled their bodies.
27. Ferocious dragons she clothed with terror,
28. She crowned them with fear-inspiring glory (and) made them like gods,
29. So that [they] might cause him who would look upon them to perish from terror,
30. So that their bodies might leap forward and none turn back their breasts.
31. She set up the viper, the dragon, and the *laḫâ[mu]*,
32. The great lion, the mad dog, and the scorpion-man,
33. Driving storm demons, the dragonfly, and the bison,
34. Bearing unsparing weapons, unafraid of battle.
35. Powerful are her decrees, irresistible are they.

---

mixing wine with spices before drinking it (cf. Ps. 75:9; Prov. 9:2; 23:30; Julian Obermann, *Ugaritic Mythology* [New Haven, 1948], p. 10; and Pliny *Naturalis historia* xiv. 19. 5). Cf. also the Greek custom of mixing wine with water in order to decrease its strength (Herodotus vi. 84). That the gods were to imbibe the wine is here taken for granted and is indicated by ll. 135–36.

TABLET III—*Continued*

36. Altogether(?) eleven (kinds of monsters) of this sort she brought [into being].
37. Of those among the gods, her first-born, who formed her [assembly],
38. She exalted Kingu; in their midst she made [him gr]eat.
39. To march at the head of the army, to [direct the forces],
40. [To rai]se the weapons for the engagement, to la[unch the attack],
41. The high com[mand of the b]attle,
42. [She intrusted] to his hand; she caused him to sit [in the assembly], (saying:)
43. '[I have ca]st the spell for thee, [I have made thee great] in the assembly of the gods.
44. The dominion over all the gods [I have given] into thy hand.
45. [Mayest] thou be highly exalted, [thou], my unique spouse!
46. May thy names become greater than (those of) [the [Anunnaki]]!'
47. She gave him the tablet of destinies, she fastened (it) upon his breast, (saying:)
48. 'As for thee, thy command shall not be changed, the word of thy mouth shall be dependable!'
49. Now when Kingu had been exalted (and) had received supreme dominion,
50. They decreed the destinies of the gods, her sons, (saying:)
51. 'May the opening of your mouths quiet the fire-god!
52. May thy overpowering poison vanquish the (opposing) might!'
53. I sent Anu, (but) he could not face her.
54. Nudimmud (also) was afraid and turned back.
55. (Then) Marduk, the wisest of the gods, your son, came forward.
56. His heart prompted (him) to face Tiᵖâmat.
57. He opened his mouth (and) said to me:
58. 'If I am indeed to be your avenger,
59. To vanquish Tiᵖâmat and to keep you alive,
60. Convene the assembly and proclaim my lot supreme.

TABLET III—*Continued*

61. When ye are joyfully seated together in the Court of Assembly,
62. May I through the utterance of my mouth determine the destinies, instead of you.
63. Whatever I create shall remain unaltered,
64. The command of my lips shall not return (void), it shall not be changed.'
65. Hasten to me (then) and speedily fix for him your destiny,
66. That he may go to meet your powerful enemy!" ' "
67. Kaka went and pursued his way.
68. Before Laḫmu and Laḫamu, the gods his ancestors,
69. He prostrated himself and kissed the ground at their feet;
70. He sat up, stood forth, and said to them:
71. "Anshar, your son, has sent me.
72. The command of his heart he has charged me to convey,
73. Saying: 'Tiʾâmat, our bearer, hates us.
74. She held a meeting and raged furiously.
75. All the gods went over to her;
76. Even those whom ye have created march at her side.
77. They separated themselves(?) and went over to the side of Tiʾâmat;
78. They were angry, they plotted, not resting day or night;
79. They took up the fight, fuming and raging;
80. They held a meeting and planned the conflict.
81. Mother Ḫubur, who fashions all things,
82. Added (thereto) irresistible weapons, bearing monster serpents
83. Sharp of tooth and not sparing the fang(?).
84. With poison instead of blood she filled their bodies.
85. Ferocious dragons she clothed with terror,
86. She crowned them with fear-inspiring glory (and) made them like gods,
87. So that he who would look upon them should perish from terror,
88. So that their bodies might leap forward and none turn back their breasts.

TABLET III—*Continued*

89. She set up the viper,[63] the dragon,[63] and the *laḫâmu,*
90. The great lion,[63] the mad dog,[63] and the scorpion-man,
91. Driving storm demons, the dragonfly, and the bison,
92. Bearing unsparing weapons, unafraid of battle.
93. Powerful are her decrees, irresistible are they.
94. Altogether(?) eleven (kinds of monsters) of this sort she brought into being.
95. Of those among the gods, her first-born, who formed her assembly,
96. She exalted Kingu; in their midst she made him great.
97. To march at the head of the army, to direct the forces,
98. To raise the weapons for the engagement, to launch the attack,
99. The high command of the battle,
100. She intrusted to his hand; she caused him to sit in the assembly, (saying:)
101. "I have cast the spell for thee, I have made thee great in the assembly of the gods.
102. The dominion over all the gods I have given into thy hand.
103. Mayest thou be highly exalted, thou, my unique spouse!
104. May thy names become greater than (those of) the Anunna[ki]!"
105. She gave him the tablet of destinies, [she fastened (it) upon his breast], (saying:)
106. "As for thee, thy command shall not [be changed, the word of thy mouth shall be dependable]!"
107. Now when Kingu had been exa[lted (and) had received supreme dominion],
108. [They decreed] the des[tinies] to the gods, her sons, (saying:)
109. "[May] the opening of your mouths [quiet the fire-god]!
110. [May] thy overpowering poison [vanquish] the (opposing) mi[ght]!"
111. I sent Anu, (but) he [could] not [face her].
112. Nudimmud (also) was afraid and [turned back].

[63] A variant has the plural.

TABLET III—*Continued*

113. (Then) Marduk, the wisest of [the gods, your son], came forward.
114. [His heart prompted (him)] to face Ti͗âmat.
115. He opened his mouth (and) [said to me]:
116. "If I am indeed to be [your avenger],
117. To vanquish Ti͗âmat (and) [to keep you alive],
118. Convene the assembly and [proclaim my lot supreme].
119. [When ye are joyfully seated together] in the Court of Assembly,
120. [May I] through the utterance of my mouth [determine the destinies], instead of [you].
121. Whatever I create shall remain unaltered,
122. The command of [my lips] shall not return (void), it shall [not be] changed."
123. Hasten to me (then) and speedily [fix for him] your destiny,
124. [That he may] go to meet your powerful enemy!' "
125. When Laḫḫa[64] (and) Laḫâmu heard (this), they cried aloud;
126. All the Igigi wailed painfully:
127. "What has happened that she has come to [such a de]cision?
128. We do not understand Ti͗âmat's ac[tion]!"
129. They gathered together and departed,
130. All the great gods who determine [the destinies].
131. They entered into the presence of Anshar and filled [the Court of Assembly];
132. They kissed one another [as they came together] in the assembly;
133. They conversed (and) [sat down] to a banquet.
134. They ate bread (and) prepared w[ine].
135. The sweet wine dispelled their fears;[65]

---

[64] I.e., Laḫmu.

[65] Reading *ú-sa-an-ni pít-ra-di-shu-[un]* and regarding *usannî* as an Assyrian form for *ushtannî*. We may compare here the phrase *shanû sha ṭêmi*, for which see Meissner in *Mitteilungen der altorientalischen Gesellschaft*, XI, Heft 1/2 (1937), 73 f.

TABLET III—*Continued*

136. [Their] bod[ies] swelled as they drank the strong drink.
137. Exceedingly carefree were they, their spirit was exalted;[66]
138. For Marduk, their avenger, they decreed the destiny.[67]

CATCH LINE

They erected for him a lordly throne-dais.

TABLET IV

1. They erected for him a lordly throne-dais,[68]
2. And he took his place before his fathers to (receive) sovereignty.
3. "Thou art (the most) important among the great gods;
4. Thy destiny is unequaled, thy command is (like that of) Anu.[69]
5. Marduk, thou art (the most) important among the great gods,
6. Thy destiny is unequaled, thy command is (like that of) Anu.
7. From this day onward thy command shall not be changed.
8. To exalt and to abase—this shall be thy power!
9. Dependable shall be the utterance of thy mouth, thy command shall not prove vain.
10. None among the gods shall infringe upon thy prerogative.[70]
11. Maintenance is the requirement of the sanctuaries of the gods;
12. And so at (each) place of their shrines shall be appointed a place for thee.
13. Marduk, thou art our avenger;
14. To thee we have given kingship over the totality of the whole universe,

[66] Contrast this passage with Tablets II: 86–91 and III: 125–28.

[67] I.e., they made him lord of the gods, in conformity with his demands (Tablets II: 122–29 and IV: 1–18).

[68] With this translation of *parakku* cf. Landsberger in *Zeitschrift für Assyriologie*, XLI (1933), 292–96.

[69] The sky-god and at one time the highest god of the pantheon.

[70] *Lit.*: overstep thy boundary.

TABLET IV—*Continued*

15. So that when thou sittest in the assembly, thy word shall be exalted.
16. May thy weapons not miss, may they smite thy foes.
17. O lord, preserve the life of him who puts his trust in thee;
18. But as for the god who has espoused evil, pour out his life!"[71]
19. Then they placed a garment in their midst;
20. To Marduk, their first-born, they said:
21. "Thy destiny,[72] O lord, shall be supreme among the gods.
22. Command to destroy and to create, (and) they shall be!
23. By the word of thy mouth, let the garment be destroyed;
24. Command again, and let the garment be whole!"
25. He commanded with his mouth, and the garment was destroyed.
26. He commanded again, and the garment was restored.[73]
27. When the gods his fathers beheld the power of his word,[74]
28. They were glad (and) did homage, (saying:) "Marduk is king!"
29. They bestowed upon him the scepter, the throne, and the royal robe(?);
30. They gave him an irresistible weapon smiting the enemy, (saying:)
31. "Go and cut off the life of Tiᵃmat.
32. May the winds carry her blood to out-of-the-way places."[75]
33. After the gods his fathers had determined the destiny of Bêl,[76]

[71] The expression "to pour out the life of someone" is taken from the pouring-out or shedding of blood, the seat of the element of life.

[72] Thy power and authority.

[73] There is no proof that Marduk reduced the garment to nothing in the strict sense and that he then re-created it out of nothing. As far as available evidence is concerned, the dogma of a *creatio ex nihilo* was not shared by the Babylonians and Assyrians. The import of this passage in all likelihood is simply that at Marduk's first command the garment was torn to shreads and that at his second command it was fully restored to its former condition.

[74] *Lit.*: the issue of his mouth.

[75] Cf. l. 132.

[76] I.e., Marduk.

TABLET IV—*Continued*

34. They set him on the road—the way to success and attainment.
35. He made a bow and decreed (it) as his weapon;
36. An arrowhead he put (on the arrow and) fastened the bowstring to it.[77]
37. He took up the club and grasped (it) in his right hand;
38. The bow and the quiver he hung at his side.
39. The lightning he set before him;
40. With a blazing flame he filled his body.[78]
41. He made a net to inclose Tiᵓâmat within (it),
42. (And) had the four winds take hold that nothing of her might escape;
43. The south wind, the north wind, the east wind, (and) the west wind,
44. The gift of his (grand)father, Anu, he caused to draw nigh to the border(s) of the net.
45. He created the *imḫullu:* the evil wind, the cyclone, the hurricane,
46. The fourfold wind, the sevenfold wind, the whirlwind, the wind incomparable.
47. He sent forth the winds which he had created, the seven of them;
48. To trouble Tiᵓâmat within, they arose behind him.
49. The lord raised the rain flood,[79] his mighty weapon.
50. He mounted (his) irresistible, terrible storm chariot;
51. He harnessed for it a team of four and yoked (them) to it,
52. The Destructive, the Pitiless, the Trampler,[80] the Flier.
53. They were sharp of tooth, bearing poison;

[77] To the bow.

[78] The scene is reminiscent of Exod. 19:16–18.

[79] The term *abûbu*, "rain flood," "cloudburst," or the like, has been treated by Jensen in *Reallexikon der Assyriologie*, I, 11–13. As Jensen points out, there are passages in which *abûbu* denotes also a mythical being of some kind. But there is no warrant for rendering this expression by "dragon" (as against W. F. Albright in the *Journal of Biblical Literature*, LXII [1943], 370). The fact that a passage in Sargon's Eighth Campaign speaks of an *abûbu* with wings proves nothing for the dragon nature of the *abûbu*. Cf. the winged bulls of Assyria, the winged horse Pegasus of Greek mythology, and the six-winged angels in the sixth chapter of Isaiah.

[80] See Landsberger in *Zeitschrift für Assyriologie*, XLIII (1936), 75, "Z. 60."

TABLET IV—*Continued*

54. They knew how to destroy, they had learned to overrun;
55. [. . . .] they [smo]te, they were frightful in battle;
56. To the left [. . . .].
57. He was clad in a terrifying coat of mail;
58. Terror-inspiring splendor he wore on his head.
59. The lord took a direct (route) and pursued his way;
60. Toward the place of raging Tiᵓâmat he set his face.
61. Between his lips he holds [a talisman(?)] of red paste;
62. An herb to destroy the poison he grasped in his hand.
63. Then the gods r[un] about him, the gods run about him;
64. The gods his fathers run about him, the gods run about him.
65. The lord drew nigh to look into the heart of Tiᵓâmat,
66. (And) to see the plan of Kingu, her spouse.
67. As he[81] gazes, (Kingu) is confused in his plan;
68. Destroyed is his will and disordered his action.
69. As for the gods his helpers, who were marching at his side,
70. When they saw the valiant hero, their vision became blurred.
71. Tiᵓâmat set up a ⌜roar(?)⌝ without turning her neck,
72. Upholding with her li[ps] (her) meanness(?) (and) rebellion:[82]
73. "⌜. . . .⌝ . . have the gods risen up to thee?
74. (Or) have they gathered from their [place] to thy place?"[83]
75. Then the lord [raised] the rain flood, his mighty weapon.[84]
76. [As for T]iᵓâmat, who was furious, thus he answered her:
77. "[In arrogance(?)] thou art risen (and) hast highly exalted thyself(?).
78. [Thou hast caused] thy heart to plot the stirring-up of conflict.
79. [. . . .] the sons treat their fathers unjustly;

[81] Marduk.

[82] Cf. Jensen in *Orientalistische Literaturzeitung*, Vol. XXVIII (1925), col. 23.

[83] I interpret Tiᵓâmat's remark to mean: "Have the gods *ascended* to your level or have they *descended* to your level?"

[84] For ll. 75–83 see the fragment published by E. F. Weidner in *Archiv für Orientforschung*, III (1926), 122–24.

TABLET IV—*Continued*

80. (And) thou, their bearer, dost hate (them) wi[thout cause(?)].
81. Thou hast exalted Kingu to be [thy] spouse;
82. Thine illegal [authority] thou hast set up in place of the authority of Anu.
83. [Against] Anshar, the king of the gods, thou seekest evil,
84. And hast proven thy wickedness [against the god]s my fathers.
85. Let thine army be equipped! let them be girded with thy weapons!
86. Come thou forth (alone) and let us, me and thee, do single combat!"
87. When Ti'âmat heard this,
88. She became like one in a frenzy (and) lost her reason.
89. Ti'âmat cried out loud (and) furiously,
90. To the (very) roots her two legs shook back and forth.
91. She recites an incantation, repeatedly casting her spell;
92. As for the gods of battle, they sharpen their weapons.
93. Ti'âmat (and) Marduk, the wisest of the gods, advanced against one another;
94. They pressed on[85] to single combat, they approached for battle.
95. The lord spread out his net and enmeshed her;
96. The evil wind, following after, he let loose in her face.
97. When Ti'âmat opened her mouth to devour him,
98. He drove in the evil wind, in order that (she should) not (be able) to close her lips.
99. The raging winds filled her belly;
100. Her belly became distended,[86] and she opened wide her mouth.
101. He shot off an arrow, and it tore her interior;
102. It cut through her inward parts, it split (her) heart.
103. When he had subdued her, he destroyed her life;

[85] Reading *id-lu-pu*.

[86] This translation I owe to Landsberger, who, in one of his contributions to the Assyrian Dictionary files of the Oriental Institute, reads *in-ni-sil*, from *esêlu*, which he renders "aufblähen," "schwellen." R. Campbell Thompson in *Revue d'assyriologie*, XXVI (1929), 54, took this verb in the sense of "to be constricted, compressed."

TABLET IV—*Continued*

104. He cast down her carcass (and) stood upon it.

105. After he had slain Tiᵓâmat, the leader,

106. Her band broke up, her host dispersed.[87]

107. As for the gods her helpers, who marched at her side,

108. They trembled for fear (and) faced about.[88]

109. They tried to break away to save their lives,

110. (But) they were completely surrounded, (so that) it was impossible to flee.

111. He imprisoned them and broke their weapons.

112. In the net they lay and in the snare they were;

113. They hid in the corners (and) were filled with lamentation;

114. They bore his wrath, being confined in prison.

115. As for the eleven (kinds of) creatures which she had laden with terror-inspiring splendor,

116. The host of demons that marched ⌜impetuously before⌝ her,

117. He cast (them) into fetters (and) [tied(?)] their arms [together(?)];

118. With (all) their resistance, [he tr]ampled (them) underfoot.

119. As for Kingu, who had become chief among them,

120. He bound him and counted him among the dead gods.[89]

---

[87] The following lines treat of three different kinds of gods composing Tiᵓâmat's fighting force: ll. 107–14 speak of the gods who had gone over to Tiᵓâmat; ll. 115–18 refer to the eleven kinds of divine monsters which Tiᵓâmat had created; and ll. 119–21 deal with Kingu, Tiᵓâmat's new husband and general. All these gods were imprisoned and hence are called the "captive gods" (l. 127).

[88] *Lit.*: they turned their back.

[89] See A. L. Oppenheim in *Orientalia*, XVI (New ser., 1947), 229, n. 2. By the "dead" gods is doubtless meant all the imprisoned deities mentioned in ll. 107–21. They were not actually put to death but had been vanquished and reduced to extreme misery, which the Mesopotamians regarded as tantamount to death. That they were not killed is clear from l. 127, according to which Marduk "strengthened his hold upon the captive gods," and from Tablet VI, which pictures Kingu as being still among the living. In fact, the gods referred to in the opening line of Tablet VI are in all likelihood the imprisoned deities enumerated in Tablet IV: 107–21. They are not called "captive gods" or the like in Tablet VI presumably because their identity was unmistakable in the light of the now missing portion of Tablet V. It was upon them that "the service of the gods" had originally been imposed; but, after listening to their petition, Marduk, "the merciful" (Tablet VII: 30), decided to create man, to place *him* in charge of this service, to relieve the defeated

TABLET IV—*Continued*

121. He took from him the tablet of destinies, which was not his rightful possession.
122. He sealed (it) with (his) seal and fastened (it) on his breast.[90]
123. After he had vanquished (and) subdued his enemies,
124. Had overpowered the arrogant foe like a bull(?),
125. Had fully established Anshar's victory over the enemy,
126. Had attained the desire of Nudimmud,[91] the valiant Marduk
127. Strengthened his hold upon the captive gods;
128. And then he returned to Tiᵓâmat, whom he had subdued.
129. The lord trod upon the hinder part of Tiᵓâmat,
130. And with his unsparing club he split (her) skull.
131. He cut the arteries of her blood
132. And caused the north wind to carry (it) to out-of-the-way places.
133. When his fathers[92] saw (this), they were glad and rejoiced
134. (And) sent him dues (and) greeting-gifts.
135. The lord rested, examining her dead body,
136. To divide the abortion[93] (and) to create ingenious things (therewith).
137. He split her open like a mussel(?) into two (parts);
138. Half of her he set in place and formed the sky (therewith) as a roof.
139. He fixed the crossbar (and) posted guards;
140. He commanded them not to let her waters escape.[94]

---

gods and by this means and the application of his holy incantation to restore the "dead" gods to life (Tablets VI:1–34 and 152–53; VII:26–29). For references to other legends concerning Kingu see S. Langdon, *The Babylonian Epic of Creation* (Oxford, 1923), p. 144, n. 5, and Knut Tallqvist, *Akkadische Götterepitheta* (Helsinki, 1938), p. 437.

[90] *Lit.*: he seized (it) with his breast.

[91] Marduk carried out his father's plan and thus succeeded where Ea had failed.

[92] I.e., Anshar, Ea, and the other older gods.

[93] See Thureau-Dangin in *Revue d'assyriologie*, XIX (1922), 81 f. The monstrous corpse of Tiᵓâmat is here compared to a thing as repulsive as an abortion.

[94] I.e., the waters of Tiᵓâmat which were contained in that half of her body which Marduk used in the construction of the sky.

TABLET IV—*Continued*

141. He crossed the heavens and examined the regions.
142. He placed himself opposite the *Apsû*, the dwelling of Nudimmud.
143. The lord measured the dimensions of the *Apsû*,
144. And a great structure, its[95] counterpart, he established, (namely,) Esharra,
145. The great structure Esharra which he made as a canopy.[96]
146. Anu, Enlil, and Ea he (then) caused to inhabit their residences.[97]

CATCH LINE

He created stations for the great gods.

COLOPHON

1. 146 lines. Fourth tablet of *Enûma elish*. Incomplete.[98]
2. Written according to a tablet whose text was crossed out.
3. Nabû-bêlshu, (the son of) Naʾid-Marduk, the son of a smith, wrote (it) for the life of his soul
4. And the life of his house and deposited (it) in (the temple) Ezida.

[95] I.e., the counterpart of the *Apsû*.

[96] Esharra in this passage is a poetic designation of the earth, which is pictured as a great structure, in the shape of a canopy, placed over the *Apsû*. For this interpretation see Jensen, *Die Kosmologie der Babylonier* (Strassburg, 1890), pp. 195–201, and *Assyrisch-babylonische Mythen und Epen* (Berlin, 1900), pp. 344 f.; Morris Jastrow, Jr., *The Religion of Babylonia and Assyria* (Boston, 1898), pp. 430–32. The import of the second half of this line cannot be that Marduk at this time created the sky, for the sky was made already in l. 138.

[97] Now that heaven and earth were completed, Anu, Enlil, and Ea, at the instance of Marduk, occupied their residences, which must not be confused with the stations mentioned in the next tablet, for these were set up later, as is evident from Tablet V : 7–8. Anu occupied the sky, Enlil the air and the surface of the earth, and Ea the sweet waters in and on the earth. Enlil was god not only of the air but also of the surface of the earth, as is attested by the fact that in the Gilgamesh Epic, Tablet XI : 41, Babylonia (or a certain area thereof) is called "the land of Enlil," and by his titles "lord of the land," "lord of the whole land," "lord of the lands," and "king of the lands." Before the creation of the earth, Ea lived in his *Apsû*, the building of which is recorded in Tablet I. Now he took possession of those areas which he occupied in historic times, viz., all the sweet waters on and below the surface of the earth, his realm embracing the waters in the underground strata, the wells and springs, the rivers, lagoons, and marshes.

[98] I.e., the *series* is still incomplete; Tablets V–VII are yet to come.

TABLET V

1. He created stations for the great gods;
2. The stars their likeness(es), the signs of the zodiac, he set up.
3. He determined the year, defined the divisions;
4. For each of the twelve months he set up three constellations.
5. After he had def[ined] the days of the year [by means] of constellations,
6. He founded the station of Nîbiru[99] to make known their duties(?).[100]
7. That none might go wrong (and) be remiss,
8. He established the stations of Enlil and Ea[101] together with it.[102]
9. He opened gates on both sides,[103]
10. And made strong lock(s) to the left and to the right.
11. In the very center thereof he fixed the zenith.
12. The moon he caused to shine forth; the night he intrusted (to her).
13. He appointed her, the ornament of the night, to make known the days.
14. "Monthly without ceasing go forth[104] with a tiara.

[99] Nîbiru = Jupiter (see A. Schott in *Zeitschrift für Assyriologie*, XLIII [1936], 124–45).

[100] I.e., the duties(?) of the days.

[101] The station (i.e., the way or path) of Enlil corresponds to the northern band of the celestial vault, and that of Ea to the southern band. A variant has, probably by mistake, "Enlil and Anu." The way of Anu is the equatorial band, about sixteen and a half degrees to each side of the equator (see J. Schaumberger in F. X. Kugler, *Sternkunde und Sterndienst in Babel*, 3. Ergänzungsheft [Münster i.W., 1935], pp. 321 f.).

[102] "Together with it" means as much as "beside it," i.e., beside the station of Nîbiru, whose station lay between those of Enlil and Ea and came within the sphere of Anu (see Schott in *Zeitschrift für Assyriologie*, XLIII, 144, and Schaumberger in Kugler, *op. cit.*, p. 330).

[103] By the two sides is meant east and west, called "left and right" in the next line. The gates refer to the mythological gates at sunrise and sunset through which the sun-god was believed to come out in the morning and leave in the evening.

[104] Reading *ú-mush*, the I, 1 imperative of *namâshu*, as suggested by Meissner in *Sitzungsberichte der Preussischen Akademie der Wissenschaften* (Phil.-hist. Klasse, 1931), p. 386, n. 1.

TABLET V—*Continued*

15. At the beginning of the month, namely, of the rising o[ver] the land,
16. Thou shalt shine with horns to make known six days;
17. On the seventh day with [hal]f a tiara.
18. At the full moon thou shalt stand in opposition (to the sun), in the middle of each [month].[105]
19. When the sun has [overtaken] thee on the foundation of heaven,[106]
20. Decrease [the tiara of full] light[107] and form (it) backward.
21. [At the period of invisi]bility draw near to the way of the sun,
22. And on [the twenty-ninth] thou shalt stand in opposition to the sun a second time.[108]
23. [. . . .] omen, enter upon her way.
24. [. . . . ap]proach and render judgment.
25. [. . . .] to violate.
26. [. . . .] to me."

(*Break*)

CATCH LINE

As [Marduk] hears [the word]s of the gods.

COLOPHON

Fifth tablet (of) *Enûma elish.*
Palace of Ashurbanipal, king of the world, king of Assyria.

---

[105] The date of the appearance of the full moon in the Babylonian sense fluctuates between the twelfth and the sixteenth of the month (see Schaumberger in Kugler, *op. cit.*, p. 261).

[106] I.e., on the horizon.

[107] Reading with some doubt [*agî tashri*]*ḫti.*

[108] S. Langdon, *The Babylonian Epic of Creation* (Oxford, 1923), p. 162, n. 2: "The Babylonians spoke of two oppositions of the moon, the first (in line 18) at the full moon directly opposite the sun, and the second when the moon stood between the earth and the sun at the end of the period of invisibility (28th–29th days of the month), just before the sun overtakes it on the western horizon before sunset (new moon)."

TABLET VI

1. As [Mar]duk hears the words of the gods,[109]
2. His heart prompts (him) to create ingenious things.
3. He conveys his idea to Ea,
4. Imparting the plan [which] he had conceived in his heart:
5. "Blood[110] will I form and cause bone to be;
6. Then will I set up *lullû*, 'Man' shall be his name!
7. Yes, I will create *lullû*: Man!
8. (Upon him) shall the services of the gods be imposed that they may be at rest.
9. Moreover, I will ingeniously arrange the ways of the gods.[111]
10. They shall be honored alike, but they shall be divided into two (groups)."
11. Ea answered him, speaking a word to him,
12. To make him change his mind concerning the relief of the gods:
13. "Let a brother of theirs be delivered up;
14. Let him be destroyed and men be fashioned.
15. Let the great gods assemble hither,
16. Let the guilty one be delivered up, and let them[112] be established."
17. Marduk assembled the great gods,
18. Ordering (them) kindly (and) giving instructions.
19. The gods pay attention to his word,
20. As the king addresses a word to the Anunnaki, (saying:)
21. "Verily, the former thing which we declared unto you has come true![113]

[109] For ll. 1–28 cf. the fragment published by Erich Ebeling in *Mitteilungen der altorientalischen Gesellschaft*, XII, Heft 4 (1939), 26. With the entire tablet are to be compared W. von Soden's notes in *Zeitschrift für Assyriologie*, XLVII (1941), 3–8.

[110] *Da-mi* = *dâmî* or *dâmê*, i.e., the acc. pl. of *dâmu* (cf. Hebrew *dāmîm*, "bloods" or "drops of blood").

[111] Cf. ll. 39–44. By the "ways" of the gods is meant the relationships and positions of the gods.

[112] The other gods who had gone over to Tiʾâmat.

[113] In this line Marduk refers to his prediction of Tiʾâmat's speedy end (Tablet II:106–15).

TABLET VI—*Continued*

22. (Also now) I speak the truth under an oath(?) by myself.[114]
23. Who was it that created the strife,
24. And caused Tiʾâmat to revolt and prepare for battle?
25. Let him who created the strife be delivered up;
26. I will make him bear his punishment, be ye at rest."
27. The Igigi, the great gods, answered him,[115]
28. The "king of the gods of heaven and earth," the counselor of the gods, their lord:
29. "Kingu it was who created the strife,[116]
30. And caused Tiʾâmat to revolt and prepare for battle."
31. They bound him and held him before Ea;
32. Punishment they inflicted upon him by cutting (the arteries of) his blood.
33. With his blood they created mankind;
34. He[117] imposed the services of the gods (upon them) and set the gods free.[118]
35. After Ea, the wise, had created mankind,
36. (And) they had imposed the service of the gods upon them[119]—
37. That work was not suited to (human) understanding;
38. In accordance with the ingenious plans of Marduk did Nudimmud[120] create (it)—,
39. Marduk, the king, divided
40. The totality of the Anunnaki above and below;[121]
41. He assigned (them) to Anu, to guard his decrees.
42. Three hundred he set in the heavens as a guard.
43. Moreover, the ways of (the gods of) the earth he defined.

[114] Marduk, shifting from the *pluralis majestatis* to the first person singular, here alludes to the promise he is about to make in l. 26.

[115] According to l. 20, Marduk addressed his question to the Anunnaki; but here the Igigi furnish the answer. The names "Anunnaki" and "Igigi" are either used interchangeably in this passage or the Igigi are included among the Anunnaki. On these two groups of gods see Tallqvist, *op. cit.*, pp. 255 and 323.

[116] For ll. 29–51 see Weidner's article in *Archiv für Orientforschung*, XI (1936/37), 72–74.

[117] Ea.

[118] The other rebel gods.

[119] *Lit.*: upon him (viz., upon man).

[120] I.e., Ea.

[121] Cf. l. 10.

TABLET VI—*Continued*

44. In heaven and in earth six hundred he caused to dwell.[122]
45. After he had issued all the decrees,
46. (And) to the Anunnaki of heaven and earth had allotted their portions,
47. The Anunnaki opened their mouth(s)
48. And said to Marduk, their lord:
49. "Now, O lord, who hast established our freedom from compulsory service,[123]
50. What shall be the sign of our gratitude before thee?
51. Come, let us make (something) whose name shall be called 'Sanctuary.'
52. It shall be a dwelling for our rest at night; come, let us repose therein!
53. There let us erect a throne dais, a seat with a back support!
54. On the day that we arrive,[124] we will repose in it."[124a]
55. When Marduk heard this,
56. His countenance shone exceedingly, [lik]e the day, (and he said:)
57. '"So(?)'[1] shall Babylon be, whose construction ye have desired;
58. Let its brickwork be fashioned, and call (it) a sanctuary."
59. The Anunnaki wielded the hoe.
60. One year they made bricks for it;
61. When the second year arrived,
62. They raised the head of Esagila[125] on high, level with the *Apsû*.[126]
63. After they had built the lofty stagetower of the *Apsû*,
64. They established an abode therein(?) for Marduk, Enlil, (and) Ea.
65. He[127] sat down before them in majesty,

[122] By the Anunnaki of the earth are meant the Anunnaki of the underworld.

[123] On this translation of *shubarrû* see F. M. Th. Böhl in *Mitteilungen der altorientalischen Gesellschaft*, XI, Heft 3 (1937), 18.

[124] For the New Year's festival.   [124a] In the sanctuary.

[125] The temple of Marduk with its stagetower.

[126] The meaning of this line appears to be that the foundation of Esagila reached down as far as the waters of the *Apsû*. Hence the stagetower could be called "the lofty stagetower of the *Apsû*" (l. 63).

[127] Marduk.

TABLET VI—*Continued*

66. As from the base of Esharra they look(ed) up to its horns.[128]
67. After they had completed the construction of Esagila,
68. The Anunnaki built themselves shrines.
69. ⌈. . . . all⌉ of them were gathered.
70. ⌈They sat⌉ in the elevated shrine which they had built as his dwelling.
71. He had the gods his fathers sit down to a banquet.
72. "Here is Babylon, your favorite dwelling place.
73. Make music in [its] place (and) be seated on its square(?)."
74. When the great gods had sat down,
75. The beer jug they set on, while they were seated at the banquet.
76. After they had made music in it,
77. They held a service of supplication in awe-inspiring(?) Esagila.
78. The (laws pertaining to) portents were fixed, all the omens.
79. The stations in heaven and earth the gods allotted, all of them.
80. The fi[fty] great gods took their seats;
81. And then the seven gods (determining) the destinies set three hundred (gods) [in the heavens].
82. Enlil lifted up the b[ow, his[129]] we[apon(?)], (and) laid (it) before them.
83. The net which he had made the gods his fathers beheld.
84. When they saw the bow, how skilfully its construction was made,
85. His fathers praised the work which he had done.
86. Anu lifted (it) up and spoke in the assembly of the gods.
87. He kissed the bow, (saying:) "This [. . . .]."

[128] At the end of Tablet IV, as we have seen, "Esharra" occurs as a name for the earth. Here it probably designates the room on top of the temple tower, as in the case of Anu's temple tower in Uruk (on which see Falkenstein, *Topographie von Uruk* [Leipzig, 1941], p. 27). According to the annals of Ashurbanipal also the temple tower at Susa had horns, consisting of shining copper (see Sidney Smith in the *Journal of the Royal Asiatic Society*, 1928, p. 858). For a pictorial representation of such horns see Meissner, *Babylonien und Assyrien*, I (Heidelberg, 1920), 311.

[129] Marduk's.

TABLET VI—*Continued*

88. He named the names of the bow as follows:
89. "Longwood is the first (name); the seco[nd is . . .];
90. Its third name is Bow-Star; in heaven [. . . .]."
91. He established its place [. . . .].
92. After [he had determined] the destinies of [the Bow-Star],
93. He set up a throne [. . . .].
94. A second one(?) in heaven [. . . .].
95. [The great gods ga]thered [. . . .].
96. [. . . .] Marduk [. . . .].
97–98. (*Almost completely destroyed*)
99. He gave him [. . . .].
100. For the dominion over the go[ds(?) . . . .].
101. He made surpassing [. . . .].
102. For his names [. . . .].
103. He opened [his] mouth [and . . . .]:
104. "At his command [. . . .] shall be supreme [. . . .].
105. Let him be highly exalted ⌜. . . .⌝.
106. Let his high-priesthood be supreme ⌜. . . .⌝.
107. Let him exercise shepherdship over mankind, [his] crea-[tures(?)].
108. Throughout the days to come let them, without forgetting, make mention of [his deeds(?)].
109. Let him establish great offerings for his fathers;
110. Let them provide for their maintenance (and) let them take care of their sanctuaries.[130]
111. May he provide (the gods) with burnt offerings to smell; their incantations may be ⌜. . . .⌝.
112. A likeness of what he made(?) in heaven [let him make(?)] on earth.
113. Let him teach mankind to ⌜fear him(?)⌝.
114. Let the subjects be ever mindful of their god (and) their goddess.
115. At the opening of his mouth, let them pay attention to (their) goddess.
116. Let offerings be brought for their god (and) their goddess;

---

[130] Reading esh-⌜ri⌝-su-un (with Landsberger *apud* von Soden in *Zeitschrift für Assyriologie*, XL, 227).

TABLET VI—*Continued*

117. Let their god be not forgotten, (but) let them support (him).
118. Let them make their land shine by building shrines for themselves.
119. Let mankind stand (in awe) before our god.
120. As for us, by as many a name as we have called (him), he shall be our god.[131]
121. Come, let us proclaim his fifty names![132]
122. Let his ways shine forth in glory, let his deeds be corresponding.
123. *Marduk* (is the name) which Anu, his (grand)father, called him from his birth;
124. The provider of pasture land and drinking places, who fills their stalls with plenty;
125. Who with his weapon, the rain flood, overcame the enemies;
126. Who saved the gods his fathers in distress.
127. Verily, the sun-child of the gods, the radiant one, is he![133]
128. In the brightness of his bright light let them walk about constantly.
129. (Upon) the people, whom he created . . . . ,
130. He[134] imposed the services of the gods, and they were set at ease.
131. At his command let there be creation, destruction, alleviation, mercy;

[131] As the Babylonians had their tutelary or personal gods, on whom they depended in a special way, so the various deities of the Babylonian pantheon had their tutelary god—Marduk.

[132] The last two lines probably mean that the gods have called Marduk by the following names among themselves, i.e., that they have *decided* on these names and that they are now going to proclaim them or make them known publicly. For a discussion of the fifty names of Marduk see Böhl's article in *Archiv für Orientforschung*, XI, 191–218.

[133] A variant has: "Verily, the sun-child, who is radiant among the gods, is he!" "Sun-child" is not a new name, as we can discern from the fact that in l. 157 it is not counted as a separate name, for otherwise the total would be ten instead of nine; it is merely a further explanation of or play upon the name "Marduk" (cf. Tablet I: 101–2).

[134] *Var.*: they (i. e., Marduk and Ea).

TABLET VI—*Continued*

132. Let them look upon him.
133. *Marukka*[135] verily is *the* god, the crea[tor of every]thing;
134. Who gladdened the hearts of the Anunnaki, who put their [minds] at ease.
135. *Marutukku* verily is the refuge of the land, the pro[tection of] his [people];
136. Him the people shall praise [. . . .].
137. *Barashakushu*[136] stood up and seized the reins (of the land);
138. Wide is his heart, (all-)embracing(?) [his] mind.
139. *Lugaldimmerankia* is his name which we named in our assembly;[137]
140. The commands of his mouth we have exalted above (those of) the gods his fathers.
141. Verily, he is the lord of all the gods of heaven and earth;
142. The king at whose instruction the gods above and below shall be afraid.[138]
143. *Narilugaldimmerankia* is his name which we named; who takes care of all the gods;
144. Who in heaven and earth established our dwelling place in (the time of) trouble;
145. Who allotted stations to the Igigi and the Annunaki.
146. At (the mention of) his name the gods shall quake (and) tremble in (their) dwelling(s).
147. *Asarluḫi* is his name by which Anu, his (grand)father, called (him);
148. Verily, he is the light of the gods, the mighty prince;
149. Who, as a *shêdu* and *lamassu*[139] of the gods and of the land,
150. In mighty combat saved our dwelling in (the time of) trouble."
151. Asarluḫi they secondly called *Namtillaku*, the god who restores to life;

[135] *Var.: Maruku.*   [136] *Var.: Shudunshakushe.*

[137] *Var.: Lugaldimmerankia,* whose name let us proclaim in our assembly.

[138] For ll. 142–66 cf. the fragment published by Ebeling in *Mitteilungen der altorientalischen Gesellschaft,* XII, Heft 4 (1939), 26 f.

[139] These two expressions denote protecting genii.

TABLET VI—*Continued*

152. Who restored all the ruined gods, as though they were his own creation;

153. The lord who by his holy incantation restored the dead gods to life;

154. The destroyer of the insidious(?) enemies; come, let us extol [his] valor!

155. Asarluḫi, whose name was thirdly called *Namshub;*[140]

156. The bright god who brightens our way.

157. Anshar, Laḫmu, and Laḫâmu each proclaimed three of his names.

158. To the gods their sons they said:

159. "We have each proclaimed three of his names.

160. Like unto us, proclaim ye (also) his names."

161. The gods rejoiced and listened to their command.

162. They took counsel together in the Court of Assembly, (saying:)

163. "Of the valiant son, our avenger

164. (And) our provider, let us exalt his name!"[141]

165. So they sat down in their assembly to proclaim his destinies,[142]

166. All of them mentioning his name(s) in the holy place(?).

CATCH LINE

Asaru, the bestower of arable land, who has established [the gran]aries.

TABLET VII[143]

1. *Asaru*, the bestower of arable land, [who has established the granaries];

2. The creator of grain and legumes, who cau[ses the green herb to spring up].

[140] The poets are here apparently playing on the Sumerian term *shuba*, which is equated with the Babylonian words *ebbu*, *ellu*, and *namru*, all of which mean "bright."

[141] *Var.*: Let us exalt the name of *the* god!

[142] *Var.*: to create (his) destinies.

[143] With the entire tablet, particularly with ll. 43–130, is to be compared von Soden's article in *Zeitschrift für Assyriologie*, XLVII, 1–26.

TABLET VII—*Continued*

3. *Asaralim*, who carries weight in the house of counsel, [who excels in counsel];

4. (On whom) the gods did wait, (for) fear [had taken hold on them].

5. *Asaralimnunna*, the mighty one, the light of [the father of his begetter];

6. Who directs the decrees of Anu, Enlil, [and Ea];

7. He alone is their provider, who assigns [their dwelling places];

8. Whose spear provides abundance.

9. *Tutu*, the author of their restoration, [is he];

10. Let him purify their sanctuaries, that they [be at ease];

11. Let him create incantations for the gods that [they be at rest];

12. If they rise in anger, let them turn back [their breasts];

13. Verily, he is highly exalted in the assembly of the gods!

14. No one among the gods can e[qual] him.

15. Tutu is *Ziukinna*, the life of the host of [the gods];

16. Who established the bright heavens for the gods;

17. Who took control of their ways and assigned [their courses(?)];

18. May he not be forgotten among men, (but) [let them hold his] deeds (in remembrance).

19. Tutu they thirdly called *Ziku*, the maintainer of purification;

20. The god of the good breath (of life), the lord who hears and answers (prayer);

21. The creator of riches and plenty, the establisher of abundance;[144]

22. Who has turned all our wants into plenty;

23. Whose good breath (of life) we smelled in sore distress;

24. Let them declare, exalt, (and) make glorious his praise.

25. Tutu may the people, in the fourth place, magnify as *Agaku*;

[144] For the text of ll. 21–45 cf. A. Falkenstein, *Literarische Keilschrifttexte aus Uruk* (Berlin, 1931), No. 38, obv.

TABLET VII—*Continued*

26. The lord of the holy incantation, who restores to life the dead;
27. Who had compassion on the vanquished gods;
28. Who removed the yoke imposed upon the gods, his enemies;
29. Who created mankind to set them free;[145]
30. The merciful, in whose power it is to give life;
31. May his words endure and not be forgotten
32. In the mouths of mankind, whom his hands have created.
33. Tutu is, in the fifth (place), *Tuku;* may their mouth(s) at all times employ(?) his holy incantation;
34. Who with his holy incantation extirpated all the evil ones.
35. *Shazu,* who knows the hearts of the gods, who sees through[146] the innermost parts;
36. From whom the evildoer cannot escape;
37. The establisher of the assembly of the gods, [who] gladdens their hearts;
38. Their wide [protec]tion, the subduer of the disobedient;
39. The administrator of justice, who pu[ts an end to(?)] crooked speech;
40. Who in his place discerns falsehood and truth.
41. Shazu may they secondly exalt as *Zisi,* who sil[ences] the insurgent;
42. Who drove the benumbing fear out of the bodies of the gods his fathers.
43. Shazu is, thirdly, *Suḥrim,* who destroys all (his) enemies with (his) weapon.
44. Who frustrates their plans (and) scatters (them) to the winds;
45. Who annihilates all the wicked ones, ... ;
46. Let the gods rejoice, (but) let *them* tremble(?)!
47. Shazu is, in the fourth (place), *Suḫgurim,* who grants petitions, who created (anew) the gods his fathers;
48. Who extirpates the enemies (and) destroys their offspring;

---

[145] To set free the vanquished gods, his enemies (cf. Tablet VI:11–34).

[146] *Var.*: who saw through.

TABLET VII—*Continued*

49. Who shatters their works, not letting anything of them remain;

50. Let his name be declared (and) uttered in the land.

51. Shazu is, in the fifth (place), *Zaḥrim;* let them extol(?) (him) as the lord(?) of the living(?);

52. Who destroys all the enemies, who requites (both) good and evil;

53. Who brought all the fugitive gods back to their sanctuaries;

54. May this his name endure!

55. In the sixth (place), may they, in addition, worship Shazu everywhere as *Zaḥgurim;*

56. Who destroyed all the enemies as if in a battle.

57. *Enbilulu,* the lord who provides them with plenty, is he;

58. The mighty one, who called them by their names, who established offerings of baked goods;

59. Who regulates pasture (and) drinking places (and) has established (them) for the land;

60. Who has opened the fountains (and) has apportioned water in abundance(?).

61. Let them secondly glorify Enbilulu as *Epadun,* the lord who waters the field(?);

62. The ruler of heaven (and) earth, the establisher of furrows, who regulates the arable land and the pasture land(?),

63. The canal and (its) embankment, who designed the furrow.

64. Let them thirdly praise Enbilulu as *Gugal,* the administrator of the plantations of the gods;

65. The lord of plenty, abundance, (and) heavy crops;

66. The provider of wealth, who enriches all(?) the dwelling places;

67. The giver of emmer, who causes barley to be.

68. Enbilulu is *Ḫegal,* who stores up plenty for man's consumption;

69. Who causes abundance to rain down upon the wide earth (and) makes the green herb grow luxuriantly.

TABLET VII—*Continued*

70. *Sirsir*,[147] who heaped up a mountain over(?) Tiᵓâmat;
71. Who with his weapon dragged off (?) the body of Tiᵓâmat;
72. The guardian of the land, their faithful shepherd;
73. . . . .;
74. Who crosses the wide sea in its anger,
75. As a bridge passes over the place of conflict.
76. Sirsir they secondly called *Malaḫ*, and so forth;
77. The sea is his craft upon which he rides.
78. *Gil*, who heaps up heaps of grain, fat hills;
79. The creator of barley and emmer, who provides seed for the land.
80. *Gilma*, the establisher of the *durmaḫ* of the gods, the creator of enduring things;
81. The bond that holds the family(?) together, the provider of good things.
82. *Agilma*, the sublime, who tears off the crown, [. . . .];
83. The creator of the clouds above the waters, the establisher of [the heavens].
84. *Zulum*, who assigns the fiel[ds. . . .];
85. The giver of portions and offerings, who supe[rvises. . . .].
86. Zulum is secondly *Mummu*, the creator of heaven (and) earth, who directs the cl[ouds];
87. The god who purifies heaven and earth;
88. To whom no one among the gods is equal in power.
89. *Gishnumunab*, the creator of all men, the maker of the four regions of the earth;
90. The destroyer of the gods of Tiᵓâmat, who created mankind with their bodies(?).[148]
91. *Lugalabdubur*, the king who shattered the works of Tiᵓâmat, who took away her weapons;
92. Whose foundation is firmly established before and behind.
93. *Pagalguenna*, the first of all the lands, the one whose strength is mighty;

[147] The reading of this name is Landsberger's.

[148] According to Tablet VI:29 ff., mankind was created with the body of Kingu alone.

TABLET VII—*Continued*

94. Who is highly exalted among the gods his brothers, the lord of all of them.

95. *Lugaldurmaḫ*, the king, the bond of the gods, the lord of the *durmaḫ;*

96. Who is highly exalted in the abode of kingship, who is very prominent among the gods.

97. *Aranunna*, the counselor of Ea, the creator of the gods his fathers;

98. Whom no god whatever can equal in his princely way.

99. *Dumuduku*, whose holy dwelling is renovated in Duku;

100. Dumuduku, without whom Lugaldukuga[149] does not make a decision.

101. *Lugallanna*, the king whose might is exalted among the gods;

102. The lord, the power of Anu, who surpasses the name(?) of Anshar.

103. *Lugalugga*, who dragged off all of them into the midst of the sea;

104. Who possesses all wisdom, who has a broad understanding.

105. *Irkingu*, who dragged off Kingu into the . . . . of the battle;

106. Who controls the instructions for all, the establisher of rulership.

107. *Kinma*, the leader of all the gods, the giver of counsel;

108. At whose name the gods tremble for fear, as at the storm.

109. *Esiskur*—may he sit on a high seat in the house of prayer;

110. May the gods bring their gifts before him.

111. (From him) they receive their assignments;

112. Without him no one can create ingenious things;

113. The four (groups of) mankind are his creation;[150]

114. Besides him no god whatever knows the appointed time(?) of their days.

115. *Girru*, the establisher of the . . . of the weapon;

116. Who in (his) conflict with Ti'âmat creates ingenious things;

117. The one with a wide understanding, an intelligent mind,

[149] Enlil, the chief god of the city of Nippur.

[150] I.e., the people of the four regions of the earth: Akkad, Elam, Subartu, and Amurru.

TABLET VII—*Continued*

118. (And) an unsearchable heart, which the gods in their totality cannot fathom.
119. *Addu* shall be his name; may he cover the whole sky;
120. May his beautiful thunder be mighty(?) upon the earth;
121. May (his) thunder rend(?) the clouds and give sustenance to the people below.
122. *Asharu*, who, as his name (indicates), took care of the gods (determining) the destinies;
123. With the nocturnal rest(?) of all the gods he is intrusted.
124. *Nîbiru* shall be in control of the passages in heaven and on earth,
125. For everyone above and below who cannot find the passage enquires of him.
126. Nîbiru is his star which they caused to shine in the sky;
127. He has taken position at the solstitial point(?), may they look upon him,
128. Saying: "He who crosses the middle of the sea without resting,
129. His name shall be Nîbiru, who occupies the middle thereof;
130. May he maintain the course of the stars of heaven;
131. May he shepherd all the gods like sheep;
132. May he subdue Tiᵓâmat, may he distress her life, and may it be short!
133. Until future (generations of) men, when the (present) days have grown old,
134. May she retreat without hindrance, may she withdraw forever!"
135. Since he created the (heavenly) places (and) fashioned the firm earth,
136. Father Enlil called his name *Lord of the Lands*.
137. All the names which the Igigi proclaimed,
138. Ea heard and his spirit rejoiced,
139. Saying: "He whose names his fathers have magnified,
140. He is even as I; his name shall (therefore) be *Ea*!
141. The totality of all my rites shall he control;
142. All my ordinances shall he direct."

TABLET VII—*Continued*

143. With the name *Fifty* the great gods

144. Called (him) whose names are fifty (and thus) made his way pre-eminent.[151]

EPILOGUE

145. Let them be held in remembrance and let the first one[152] teach (them);

146. Let the wise (and) the knowing consider (them) together;

147. Let the father repeat (them) and teach (them) to his sons;

148. Let the ears (even) of shepherd and herdsman be opened (to them).[153]

149. Let (man) rejoice in Marduk, the Enlil of the gods,

150. That his land be fruitful (and) it be well with him.

151. Reliable is his word, unalterable his command;

152. The utterance of his mouth no god whatever can change.

153. He looks on and does not turn his neck;

154. When he is wroth, no god can withstand his indignation.

155. Unsearchable is his heart, (all-)embracing his mind;

156. The sinner and the transgressor are an abom[ination] before him.

157. The instructions which an ancient(?) one spoke before him(?).

(Rest too fragmentary for translation)

[151] For the translation of the last two lines cf. Jensen in *Orientalistische Literaturzeitung*, Vol. XXVIII, col. 25. "Lord of the Lands" was originally Enlil's own title. Its transfer to Marduk involved the transfer of Enlil's power and functions to the god of Babylon. This was the last of the fifty names which the gods in their assembly had decided to proclaim (Tablet VI:121). But as Ea listened to the proclamation, in which he had apparently not taken an active part, he resolved to confer his own name on Marduk, in addition to those already proclaimed by the Igigi. Since the step which Ea here took was entirely his own, the number of names proclaimed by the assembly of the gods was still fifty, which permitted the gods to call Marduk *Ḫanšâ* ("Fifty"), in token that the names which they had declared publicly were fifty. Since *Fifty* was one of Enlil's own names and since, moreover, it epitomizes and symbolizes Marduk's fifty titles, it gave the latter pre-eminence over all the other divinities of the pantheon. With the fifty names of Marduk may be compared the ninety-nine titles of Allah.

[152] Whether in time or in rank is uncertain.

[153] I.e., may even the shepherd and the herdsman receive knowledge of the names of Marduk for their enlightenment.

CHAPTER II

RELATED BABYLONIAN CREATION STORIES

A BILINGUAL VERSION OF THE CREATION OF THE WORLD BY MARDUK[1]

IN ADDITION to the cosmogony which we have just considered, we find in Babylonian literature quite a number of stories which give rather different accounts of the manner in which all things came into being. The most important one of them all is a bilingual story discovered by Hormuzd Rassam in 1882 among the ruins of the ancient city of Sippar (the modern Abu Ḥabba) and dating back to Neo-Babylonian times (sixth century B.C.). This creation account probably arose at the city of Eridu, which was located at the mouth of the Persian Gulf. Here the land of Babylonia grew from year to year through the deposition of silt carried down by the Euphrates, and that probably gave rise to the belief, expressed in the story under consideration, that the earth had originated in the same way.[2] This version has been recorded both in Sumerian and in Babylonian and forms a rather elaborate introduction to an incantation which was recited for the purification of Ezida, the temple of Nabû at Borsippa, the mythological episodes having been added to the magical formula for the purpose of increasing the potency of the spell. The central theme and objective of the creation story itself again is the justification of Marduk's position as king among the Babylonian gods. The inscription runs as follows:

---

[1] Text published by L. W. King in *Cuneiform Texts from Babylonian Tablets, etc., in the British Museum*, Vol. XIII (London, 1901), Pls. 35–38, and translated by P. Jensen, *Assyrisch-babylonische Mythen und Epen* (Berlin, 1900), pp. 38–43; King, *The Seven Tablets of Creation* (London, 1902), I, 130–39; R. W. Rogers, *Cuneiform Parallels to the Old Testament* (New York and Cincinnati, 1926), pp. 47–50; Erich Ebeling in Hugo Gressmann, *Altorientalische Texte zum Alten Testament* (Berlin and Leipzig, 1926), pp. 130 f.; and others.

[2] See A. H. Sayce in *Encyclopaedia of Religion and Ethics,* ed. James Hastings, IV (New York and Edinburgh, 1912), 128.

1. A holy house, a house of the gods in a holy place, had not been made;
2. A reed had not come forth, a tree had not been created;
3. A brick had not been laid, a brick mold had not been built;
4. A house had not been made, a city had not been built;
5. A city had not been made, a living creature had not been placed (therein);
6. Nippur had not been made, Ekur[3] had not been built;
7. Uruk had not been made, Eanna[4] had not been built;
8. The *Apsû*[5] had not been made, Eridu had not been built;
9. A holy house, a house of the gods, its dwelling,[6] had not been made;
10. All the lands were sea;
11. The spring[7] which is in the sea was a water pipe;[8]
12. Then Eridu was made, Esagila[9] was built—
13. Esagila whose foundations Lugaldukuga laid within the *Apsû*—
14. Babylon was made, Esagila was completed;[10]
15. The gods the Anunnaki he[11] created equal.
16. The holy city, the dwelling of their hearts' delight, they called (it) solemnly.
17. Marduk constructed a reed frame on the face of the waters;
18. He created dirt and poured (it) out by the reed frame.

[3] The main temple of the city of Nippur.

[4] The main temple of Uruk (the biblical Erech).

[5] Here apparently the great lagoons of the Euphrates at the Persian Gulf, where the city of Eridu was located (see R. Campbell Thompson, *The British Museum Excavations at Abu Shahrain in Mesopotamia in 1918* [Oxford, 1920], pp. 124–26).

[6] The dwelling par excellence of Eridu, i.e., the temple of Eridu.

[7] This translation of *i-nu* (= *înu*) was suggested to me by Thorkild Jacobsen. The reference is probably to the fresh-water springs in the sea around the island Baḥrain in the Persian Gulf, where "water bubbles up beneath the sea with such abundance that the women fill their jars with the spring-waters as if from the sea itself" (E. Burrows in *Orientalia*, XXX [1928], 9).

[8] The water came out in such volume as if through a water pipe.

[9] In ll. 12 and 13 Esagila is probably the name of a temple in Eridu and not the well-known temple complex in Babylon mentioned in l. 14.

[10] Line 14 seems to be a disturbing element in this context and may be a later addition by the Marduk priests at Babylon.

[11] Lugaldukuga.

19. In order to settle the gods in the dwelling of (their) hearts' delight,
20. He created mankind.
21. Aruru created the seed of mankind[12] together with him.[13]
22. He created the beasts of Sumuqan[14] (and) the living things of the steppe;
23. He created the Tigris and the Euphrates and set (them) in place;
24. Their name(s) he appropriately proclaimed.
25. He created the grass, the rush of the marsh, the reed, and the woods;
26. He created the green herb of the field;
27. The lands, the marshes, the canebrakes;
28. The cow (and) her young, the calf; the ewe (and) her lamb, the sheep of the fold;
29. The orchards and the forests;
30. The wild sheep, the wool sheep(?) . . . .
31. Lord Marduk piled up a dam[15] at the edge of the sea;
32. [. . . .] a swamp he made into dry land.[16]
33. [. . . .] he caused to be;
34. [He crea]ted [the reed(?)], he created the tree;
35. [. . . .] in the place he created;
36. [Bricks he laid, the br]ick mold he built;
37. [The house he built], the city he built;
38. [The city he made], living creatures he placed (therein);
39. [Nippur he built], Ekur he built;
40. [Uruk he built, Eann]a he built.

The rest of the obverse and approximately the first half of the reverse of the tablet are destroyed; and, when the text again sets in, we find ourselves in the midst of the incantation to which we have referred above.

[12] The "seed of mankind" means simply "mankind" (see Jensen in *Reallexikon der Assyriologie*, I [Berlin and Leipzig, 1932], 33).

[13] The Sumerian version has "together with the god," viz., Marduk.

[14] God of cattle and vegetation.

[15] The "dam" no doubt refers to the ridge at the Persian Gulf around Basra, behind which there is a depression. This ridge is said to date back to prehistoric times (Erika Techen, *Euphrat und Tigris* [Hamburg, 1934], pp. 40–45).

[16] Reading *na-ba*(!)-*la*, from *abâlu*, "to dry up."

THE CREATION OF LIVING CREATURES[17]

This fragmentary inscription, which was found by George Smith in one of the trenches dug by the excavators at Nineveh, may have belonged to King Ashurbanipal's library. The interpretation of this text is, unfortunately, rather seriously hampered by the defective character of the tablet. In general, however, it can be stated that the few lines which have been preserved deal chiefly with the creation of living things. For many years great interest has centered around the "two little ones" created by Ninigiku, another name for Ea. What is meant by these "two little ones" or "two young ones" is difficult to determine with precision, owing to the fragmentary nature of the tablet. But to see in them the first two parents of the human race is without foundation. In fact, the expressions "the creatures of the city," which may be a designation for mankind,[18] and "my family" make that assumption highly improbable. It seems quite likely, however, that the "two little ones" refers to human servants.

1. When the gods in their assembly had created [everything(?)],
2. Had fashioned the sky, had for[med the earth(?)],
3. Had brought forth living [creatu]res [. . . .],
4. [Had created] the cattle of the field, [the beasts] of the field, and the creatures of [the city(?)],
5. Afte[r they had . . . .] unto the living creatures [. . . .],
6. [And] had apporti[oned their portions(?) to the cattle of] Sumuqan and to the creatures of the city,
7. [And had . . . . a]ll creatures, the whole of creation [. . . .],
8. [. . . .] which in all my family [. . . .],
9. Ninigiku [created] two serv[ants(?)][19] . . . .].
10. He made [them more] glorious [than a]ll (other) creatures.

(Rest almost completely destroyed)

---

[17] Text published by King in *Cuneiform Texts* . . . . , Vol. XIII, Pl. 34 (D.T. 41), and translated by him in his work *The Seven Tablets of Creation*, I, 122–25; by Rogers, *op. cit.*, pp. 50 f.; Ebeling in Gressmann, *op. cit.*, p. 136; and others.

[18] Thus Arno Poebel, *Historical Texts* (Philadelphia, 1914), p. 40.

[19] *Lit.*: "two litt[le ones]" or "two youn[g ones]."

"WHEN ANU HAD CREATED THE HEAVENS"[20]

The tablet from which this cosmological passage is taken was found at Babylon. It contains a ritual for the restoration of a temple. This ritual calls for the presentation of various kinds of offerings, the singing of a number of hymns, and the recitation of the following creation story, in which Ea figures as the creator of various minor patron deities, the king, and mankind in general. Here again we have a creation story employed as a magic formula, in this instance for the purpose of keeping away the evil influence of the demons during and after the restoration of the temple, by proclaiming the might and power of the gods.[21]

24. When Anu[22] had created the heavens,
25. (And) Nudimmud[23] had built the *Apsû*, his dwelling,[24]
26. Ea nipped off clay[25] in the *Apsû;*
27. He created Kulla[26] for the restoration of [the temples];
28. He created the reed marsh and the forest for the work of [their] construction;
29. He created Ninildu,[27] Ninsimug,[28] and Arazu,[29] to complete the work of [their] con[struction];
30. He created the mountains and the seas for whatever [. . . .];
31. He created Gushkinbanda,[30] Ninagal,[31] Ninzadim,[32] and Ninkurra[33] for [their] works,

---

[20] Text published and translated by F. H. Weissbach, *Babylonische Miscellen* (Leipzig, 1903), Pl. 12 and pp. 32–34; and translated again by F. Thureau-Dangin, *Rituels accadiens* (Paris, 1921), pp. 46 f.; A. Ungnad, *Die Religion der Babylonier und Assyrer* (Jena, 1921), pp. 54 f.; Rogers, *op. cit.*, pp. 44–46; Ebeling in Gressmann, *op. cit.*, pp. 129 f.; and others.

[21] S. A. Pallis, *The Babylonian Akîtu Festival* (Copenhagen, 1926), p. 212.

[22] The sky-god.

[23] Another name for Ea.

[24] Cf. *Enûma elish*, Tablet I:71.

[25] Cf. Job 33:6: "From clay I too was nipped off."

[26] The brick-god.

[27] The god of the carpenters.

[28] A god of the smiths.

[29] Apparently the god of prayer.

[30] The god of the goldsmiths.

[31] Another god of the smiths.

[32] The god of the engravers.

[33] A goddess of the stonecutters (S. N. Kramer in the *Journal of the American Oriental Society*, LXIII [1943], 69, n. 1; Knut Tallqvist, *Akkadische Götterepitheta* [Helsinki, 1938], p. 411).

32. And their rich produce for offerings .[. . . .];
33. He created Ashnan,[34] Laḫar,[35] Siris,[36] Ningizzida, Ninezen,[37] .[. . . .],
34. To provide abundant regular offe[rings];
35. He created Umunmutamku (and) Umunmutamnak,[38] to present [their] offer[ings];
36. He created the god Kusig, the high priest of the great gods, for the performance of the rites (and) ce[remonies];
37. He created the king, for the mainten[ance of the temples];
38. [He created] mankind for the doi[ng of the service of the gods(?)].[39]

(*Rest destroyed*)

THE CREATION OF MAN[40]

The present story, according to which the goddess Mami at the behest of Enki (i.e., Ea) and other deities created man from clay mixed with the blood of a slain god, is found on a badly mutilated and weather-worn tablet of the First Babylonian Dynasty. Originally the tablet contained at least four columns of some length. Whether this episode relates to the first creation of man or whether it deals with a second creation of man, perhaps after the deluge, cannot be stated with finality. The fact that in line 8 Mami is already called "the creatress of mankind" seems to point to the latter assumption.[41] From the reverse of

[34] A grain deity.

[35] Seems to be a deity of the herd or the fold (cf. A. Deimel, *Pantheon babylonicum* [Rome, 1914], p. 162; Tallqvist, *op. cit.*, p. 347).

[36] A wine-goddess.　　　[37] Apparently two deities of vegetation.

[38] The two names appear in Babylonian as *Minâ-îkul-bêlî* ("What will my lord eat?") and *Minâ-ishtî-bêlî* ("What will my lord drink?"), designating Marduk's cook and cupbearer, respectively (cf. Poebel, *Studies in Akkadian Grammar* [Chicago, 1939], p. 119).

[39] Cf. *Enûma elish*, Tablet VI:8 and 33 f.

[40] The inscription has been published by T. G. Pinches in *Cuneiform Texts . . . .*, Vol. VI (London, 1898), Pl. 5, and by S. Langdon, *Sumerian Epic of Paradise, the Flood and the Fall of Man* (Philadelphia, 1915), Pls. III f., and has been translated by Langdon, *ibid.*, pp. 25 f.; by Ungnad, *op. cit.*, p. 55; Ebeling in Gressmann, *op. cit.*, p. 134; and again by Ebeling, *Tod und Leben nach den Vorstellungen der Babylonier* (Berlin and Leipzig, 1931), pp. 172–76.

[41] See Jensen, *Assyrisch-babylonische Mythen und Epen*, pp. 275 f., and King, *The Seven Tablets of Creation*, I, lvii, n. 1.

the tablet it is quite clear that this creation legend formed a lengthy introduction to a birth incantation. The purpose of introducing the incantation with this story obviously was to gain the help and good graces of Ninḫursag (or Mami), the goddess of birth, by recounting one of her great deeds and thus to facilitate delivery. The following lines are taken from the third column of the tablet.

1-2. (*Destroyed*)
3. "What is little he shall raise to abundance;
4. The ⌜. . .⌝ of creation(?) man shall bear."
5. The goddess they called, ⌜. . . .⌝,
6. The help(?) of the gods, the wise Mami:
7. "Thou art the mother-womb,
8. The creatress of mankind;
9. Create Man[42] that he may bear the yoke;[43]
10. That he may bear the yoke ⌜. . . .⌝.
11. The ⌜. . .⌝ of creation(?) man shall bear."
12. Nintu[44] opened her mouth
13. And said to the great gods:
14. "With me alone it is impossible to do;
15. With his help[45] there will be ⌜Man⌝.
16. He shall be the one who ⌜fears⌝ all the ⌜gods⌝.
17. Clay ⌜. . . .⌝."
18. Enki opened his mouth
19. And said to the great gods:
20. "In the month of substitution(?) and help,
21. Of the purification of the land (and) the judgment of its shepherd,
22. Let them slay a god,
23. And let the gods . . . . .
24. With his flesh and his blood
25. Let Ninḫursag mix clay.
26. God and man
27. . . . . united(?) in the clay.

(*The rest of this column is too badly damaged to be intelligible*)

[42] *Lu-ul-la-a.*
[43] Cf. *Enûma elish*, Tablet VI:8 ff.   [44] Another name for Mami.
[45] Probably the help of Enki (cf. l. 18). Reading *ri-ṣú(!)-⟨ti⟩-shu.*

ANOTHER ACCOUNT OF THE CREATION OF MAN[46]

A tablet discovered among the ruins of the city of Ashur and dating back to approximately 800 B.C. gives us still another version of the creation of man. This text consists of three columns. The first contains signs which are held by some to be musical notes but which are most likely symbols of some kind of secret writing;[47] the second contains the Sumerian version of the story of man's creation; and the third offers the Babylonian translation of it. On this tablet mention is made for the first time in Babylonian-Assyrian literature of the first two human beings and their names, Ulligarra and Zalgarra. Before each one's name is placed the sign for "deity," which means that the first ancestors of mankind were regarded as being divine at least to some degree. The reason for this conception lies, of course, in the fact that they were thought to have been created with divine blood, which, according to other sources, was mixed with clay.

OBVERSE

1. When heaven had been separated from the earth, the distant trusty twin,[48]
2. (And) the mother of the goddesses had been brought into being;
3. When the earth had been brought forth (and) the earth had been fashioned;
4. When the destinies of heaven and earth had been fixed;

---

[46] Text published by Ebeling in *Keilschrifttexte aus Assur religiösen Inhalts*, No. 4; translated by the same author in *Zeitschrift der deutschen morgenländischen Gesellschaft*, LXX (1916), 532–38; by Ungnad, *op. cit.*, pp. 56 f.; and again by Ebeling in Gressmann, *op. cit.*, pp. 134–36; and others. A good photo of the tablet has been published by S. Landersdorfer, *Die sumerischen Parallelen zur biblischen Urgeschichte* (Münster i.W., 1917), Pls. I–II. For a duplicate from Nineveh see Carl Bezold in the *Proceedings of the Society of Biblical Archaeology*, X (1887/88), Pls. I–II (between pp. 418 and 419), and T. J. Meek in *Revue d'assyriologie*, XVII (1920), 189 (82-3-23, 146); cf. also E. F. Weidner in the *American Journal of Semitic Languages and Literatures*, XXXVIII (1921/22), 209.

[47] On this point see Landsberger in *Archiv für Orientforschung*, Beiband I (1933), 170–78; cf. also C. J. Gadd in *Iraq*, IV (1937), 33–34.

[48] With the translation of this line cf. Jacobsen in the *Journal of Near Eastern Studies*, V (1946), 143, n. 24.

5. (When) trench and canal had been given (their) right courses,

6. (And) the banks of the Tigris and the Euphrates had been established,

7. (Then) Anu, Enlil, Shamash, (and) Ea,

8. The great gods,

9. (And) the Anunnaki, the great gods,

10. Seated themselves in the exalted sanctuary

11. And recounted among themselves what had been created.

12. "Now that the destinies of heaven and earth have been fixed,

13. Trench and canal have been given their right courses,

14. The banks of the Tigris and the Euphrates

15. Have been established,

16. What (else) shall we do?

17. What (else) shall we create?

18. O Anunnaki, ye great gods,

19. What (else) shall we do?

20. What (else) shall we create?"

21. The great gods who were present,[49]

22. The Anunnaki, who fix the destinies,

23. Both (groups)[50] of them, made answer to Enlil:

24. "In Uzumua,[51] the bond of heaven and earth,

25. Let us slay (two) Lamga gods.[52]

26. With their blood let us create mankind.

27. The service of the gods be their portion,

28. For all times

29. To maintain the boundary ditch,

[49] *Lit.:* who were standing (there).

[50] The Anunnaki of heaven and earth.

[51] Uzumua was a sacred area in the city of Nippur (see Meissner, *Babylonien und Assyrien*, II, 111; F. M. Th. Böhl in *Archiv für Orientforschung*, XI [1936/37], 207; and Jacobsen in the *Journal of Near Eastern Studies*, V, 136–37).

[52] The Lamga deities were craftsmen gods. The text does not give the number of gods to be slain (the repetition of the name "Lamga" does *not* express duality; see Poebel, *Grundzüge der sumerischen Grammatik* [Rostock, 1923], secs. 143 and 150). However, since only two human beings are created, it seems natural to assume that not more than two gods were killed.

30. To place the hoe and the basket[53]
31. Into their hands[54]
32. For the dwelling of the great gods,
33. Which is fit to be an exalted sanctuary,
34. To mark off field from field,
35. For all times
36. To maintain the boundary ditch,
37. To give the trench (its) right course,
38. To maintain the boundary stone(?),
39. To water the four regions of the earth(?),
40. To raise plants in abundance,
41. Rains(?) [. . . .],

REVERSE

1. To maintain the boundary(?),
2. To fill(?) the granary,
3–5. (*Destroyed*)
6. To make the field of the Anunnaki[55] produce plentifully,
7. To increase the abundance in the land,
8. To celebrate the festivals of the gods,
9. To pour out cold water
10. In the great house of the gods, which is fit to be an exalted sanctuary.
11. Ulligarra (and) Zalgarra[56]
12. Thou shalt call their names."
13. That they should increase ox, sheep, cattle, fish, and fowl,
14. The abundance in the land,
15. Enul (and) Ninul[57]
16. Decreed with their holy mouths.
17. Aruru, the lady of the gods, who is fit for rulership,
18. Ordained for them great destinies:

[53] For this translation of *ṭupshíku* see Meissner in *Mitteilungen der altorientalischen Gesellschaft*, XI, Heft 1/2 (1937), 47–49.

[54] For the purpose of building.

[55] In view of the following line, the "field of the Anunnaki" probably means the earth.

[56] Probably meaning "the establisher of abundance" and "the establisher of plenty," respectively.

[57] "The lord of abundance" and "the lady of abundance," respectively.

19. Skilled worker to produce for skilled worker (and) un-
    skilled worker for unskilled worker,[58]
20. (Springing up) by themselves like grain from the ground,[59]
21. A thing which, (like) the stars of heaven, shall not be
    changed forever.
22. Day and night
23. To celebrate the festivals of the gods
24. By themselves,
25. (These) great destinies
26. Did Anu, Enlil,
27. Ea, and Ninmaḫ,[60]
28. The great gods, decree (for them).
29. In the place where mankind was created,
30. There Nisaba[61] was firmly established.
31. Let the wise teach the mystery to the wise.[62]

A SUMERIAN CREATION ACCOUNT FROM NIPPUR[63]

Another reference to the creation of man is found on a Sumerian tablet excavated at Nippur. The inscription contains a
portion of an epitomized form of a creation story, a list of pre-
diluvian cities and their divine rulers, and an account of the
deluge. The beginning of the tablet, which originally was about
three times as large as the present fragments, is broken off, and
the first few lines that have been preserved open with the closing sentence of the speech of a creating deity. The passage dealing with the creation reads as follows:

[58] This translation of *nuᵖú* I owe to Jacobsen.

[59] With these lines cf. the Sumerian myths of the pickax and of Enki and
E-engurra, according to which the first men grew up from the earth like plants
(Jacobsen in the *Journal of Near Eastern Studies*, V, 134–37).

[60] Ninmaḫ is another name for Aruru.

[61] The goddess of grain, of the scribes, of wisdom, etc. Here, because of the next
line, she probably functions as the goddess of wisdom.

[62] This legend was meant only for the initiated, which may account for the mys-
terious signs on the first column of the tablet.

[63] Text published by Poebel, *Historical and Grammatical Texts* (Philadelphia,
1914), No. 1, and translated by the same author in his volume *Historical Texts*,
p. 17; cf. also King, *Legends of Babylon and Egypt in Relation to Hebrew Tradition*
(London, 1918), pp. 49–58.

"As for my human race, from its destruction will I cause it to be [. . . .].
For Nintu my creatures [. . . .] will I .[. . .] . . .
The people will I cause to . . . . in their settlements.
Wherever(?) he[64] may build cities, I will cause him to rest in their protection.
Let him lay the brick(s) of our houses in hallowed place(s);
Let him establish our . . . . in hallowed place(s)!"
. . . . he made straight for him;[65]
The sublime commandments and precepts he made perfect for him.
When Anu, Enlil, Enki, and Ninḫursagga[66]
Had created mankind,
The . . . . of the earth they caused the earth to produce(?);
The animals, the four-legged creatures of the field, they ingeniously brought
into being.

THE WORM AND THE TOOTHACHE[67]

Here again we have a cosmological passage which is used as
part of an incantation, in this case supplemented by medical
applications to serve as an aid to the magical charm. The cosmological material here offered purports to give the history of
the worm, which the Babylonians and Assyrians associated with
toothache.

1. After Anu had created the heaven,
2. (And) the heaven had created the earth,
3. (And) the earth had created the rivers,
4. (And) the rivers had created the canals,
5. (And) the canals had created the morass,
6. (And) the morass had created the worm,
7. The worm came weeping before Shamash,
8. His tears flowing before Ea.
9. "What wilt thou give me for my food?
10. What wilt thou give me for my drink?"
11. "I will give thee the ripe fig

[64] Man.   [65] For man.
[66] A synonym of the goddess Nintu.

[67] The inscription has been published by Thompson in *Cuneiform Texts* . . . . ,
Vol. XVII (London, 1903), Pl. 50, and in his *Assyrian Medical Texts* (London,
New York, etc., 1923), No. 25, 2:15 ff.; it has been translated by Meissner in
Mitteilungen der vorderasiatischen Gesellschaft, IX, Heft 3 (1904), 42–45; Rogers,
op. cit., pp. 52 f.; Ebeling in Gressmann, *op. cit.*, pp. 133 f.; and others. For a
Ḫurrian (or Horite) recension see Thureau-Dangin in *Revue d'assyriologie*, XXXVI
(1939), 1–10.

12. (And) the apricot."[68]
13. "What is that to me? The ripe fig
14. And the apricot!
15. Lift me up and let me dwell
16. Among the teeth and the jawbones!
17. The blood of the teeth I will suck
18. And will eat away
19. The roots of the teeth in the jawbones!"
20. Insert the needle and seize the foot (of the worm)![69]
21. Because thou hast said this, O worm,
22. May Ea smite thee with the might of
23. His hand!
24. Incantation against toothache.
25. Its ritual: Second-grade beer, . . . , and oil thou shalt mix together;
26. The incantation thou shalt recite three times thereon (and) shalt put (the mixture) on his tooth.

THE CREATION OF MOON AND SUN[70]

Here we have two short legends found on a student's practice tablet of the Neo-Babylonian period; one of them is recorded in the Sumerian language, the other in Babylonian. The former treats of the creation of the moon, while the latter refers to the creation of the sun. Together they form the introduction to a larger astrological work, as we can see from Virolleaud's book just cited.

SUMERIAN

1. When Anu, Enlil, (and) Enki, the [great] gods,
2. Through their unchangeable counsel, had established the great decrees of

[68] See Thompson, *The Assyrian Herbal* (London, 1924), pp. 178–80.

[69] This line contains instructions for the dentist, the reference apparently being to the pulling of the dental nerve (cf. A. Dávid in *Revue d'assyriologie*, XXV [1928], 97).

[70] Text published by King, *The Seven Tablets of Creation*, Vol. II, Pl. XLIX, and translated *ibid.*, I, 125 and 127; again translated by Ungnad, *op. cit.*, p. 58; Rogers, *op. cit.*, pp. 46 f.; Ebeling in Gressman, *op. cit.*, p. 136. For a duplicate see Ch. Virolleaud, *L'Astrologie chaldéenne* (Paris, 1908), *Sin*, No. I.

3. Heaven and earth (and) the crescent[71] of the moon-god,
4. To let the crescent of the moon go forth to create the month,
5. And had established (it) as a sign of heaven (and) earth,
6. (And) that the crescent of the moon in the sky might cause light to shine forth,
7. He came forth visibly(?) in the midst of heaven.

BABYLONIAN

8. When Anu, Enlil, (and) Ea,[72]
9. The great gods, through their unchangeable counsel,
10. Had established the decrees of heaven and earth,
11. (And) had intrusted to the hands of the great gods
12. The bright day (and) the new moon for the sight(?) of
13. Mankind, they beheld the sun in the gate of his going-forth.
14. In the midst of heaven and earth they shone forth[73] faithfully.

AN ADDRESS TO THE RIVER[74]

This inscription is usually included among the creation stories. In reality, however, it has nothing to do with the creation of the world. It properly belongs with the literature of hymns and prayers. The first seven or eight lines form the opening words of a water ritual performed at the river, which here is deified, although the term is not preceded by the sign for divinity.[75] There can be hardly any doubt that the river addressed in this text is the mighty, chocolate-colored Euphrates, which was

[71] On this rendition of *magur* see A. Salonen, *Die Wasserfahrzeuge in Babylonien* (Helsinki, 1939), pp. 14–15.

[72] The Ea of the Semitic Babylonians corresponds to the Enki of the Sumerians.

[73] Tentatively reading *ush-ta-pu-ú*, instead of *ush-ta-mu-ú*. The subjects are the sun and the moon.

[74] Text published by King, *The Seven Tablets of Creation*, I, 200 f.; and by Ebeling, *Keilschrifttexte aus Assur religiösen Inhalts*, No. 294; translated by King, *op. cit.*, p. 129; Ebeling, *Ein babylonischer Kohelet* (Berlin, 1922), pp. 19 f.; Ebeling in Gressmann, *op. cit.*, p. 130; and others.

[75] For further references to the deified river see Ebeling, *Tod und Leben* . . . . , p. 125; G. Dossin in *Syria*, XIX (1938), 126; and Jacobsen in the *Journal of Near Eastern Studies*, V, 139, n. 21. The concept of the deified river appears also in the literature from Ras Shamra (see J. Obermann in the *Journal of the American Oriental Society*, LXVII [1947], 198–201).

to Babylonia what the Nile was to Egypt. The Euphrates was indeed the "creator of all things" and the "river of the sanctuaries," for it was chiefly upon its water that the life and fertility of Babylonia depended, and it was from its "irresistible flood of water" that the sanctuaries drew their supplies.

1. Incantation. O thou river, (thou) creator of all things!
2. When the great gods dug thee out, they set good things upon thy bank(s).
3. Within thee Ea, the king of the deep, built his dwelling.
4. An irresistible flood of water he has presented unto thee.
5. Fire (and) wrath, splendor (and) terror
6. Ea and Marduk have presented unto thee.[76]
7. Thou judgest the cause of mankind.
8. O (thou) great river, (thou) exalted river, (thou) river of the sanctuaries,
9. Thy waters (bring) release, receive me (graciously) . . . !
10. What is in my body take away to thy bank;
11. [Cause] it to go down thy bank, cause it to go down into thy depth![77]

(*The rest is too fragmentary for translation*)

EXCERPTS FROM DAMASCIUS AND BEROSSUS

Of the main Babylonian story of creation two Greek versions were known to classical scholars long before the decipherment of cuneiform. One of them we owe to Damascius, the last of the Neo-Platonic philosophers (born in Damascus about A.D. 480). His chief work is entitled *Difficulties and Solutions of First Principles*. In this treatise he gives us the following brief summary of the Babylonian views concerning the origin of the gods and of the universe:

Of the barbarians the Babylonians seem to pass over in silence the one principle of the universe, and they assume two, Tauthe and Apasōn, making

[76] For ll. 4–6 a variant has: "He has presented unto thee heat (and) wrath, splendor (and) terror. An irresistible flood of water he has called thee. At thy word have Ea and Marduk bestowed the heat." For *immu* in the sense of "heat" see W. von Soden, *Die lexikalischen Tafelserien der Babylonier und Assyrer in den Berliner Museen* (Berlin, 1933), Pl. 13, col. v, l. 319.

[77] Cf. II Kings, chap. 5: Naaman dips himself seven times in the Jordan and is cured of his leprosy.

Apasōn the husband of Tauthe and calling her the mother of the gods. Of these was born an only-begotten son, Mōymis,[78] whom I conceive to be the mental world (νοητὸς κόσμος) proceeding from the two principles. From them another generation proceeded, Dachē and Dachos. And again a third (generation proceeded) from them, Kissarē and Assoros, of whom were born three, Anos, Illinos, and Aos. And of Aos and Daukē was born a son called Bēl, who, they say, is the fabricator of the world (δημιουργός).[79]

It is indeed remarkable how well this summary agrees with *Enûma elish;* it sounds almost like a passage taken directly out of the Babylonian epic. There are, however, a number of points in this brief résumé which merit special consideration. First, there is the identification of the names. Dachē (Δαχή) and Dachos (Δαχός) are, of course, textual corruptions for Lachē (Λαχή) and Lachos (Λαχός), corresponding to the Babylonian Laḫāmu and Laḫmu (or Laḫḫa).[80] Of the other names, Tauthe and Apasōn correspond to Tiᵓâmat and Apsû; Mumis (or Mōymis) to Mummu, the son and vizier of Apsû; Kissarē and Assoros to Kishar and Anshar; Anos to Anu, Illinos to Enlil (or Ellil); Aos to Ea; Daukē to Damkina; and Bēl to Marduk, who in the later days of Babylonian history was quite commonly known as Bêl. Second, Damascius calls Mummu "an only-begotten son" or "a single son" (μονογενὴς παῖς) of Apsû and Tiᵓâmat, i.e., while the following two generations, Laḫmu and Laḫāmu, Anshar and Kishar, issued in pairs, Mummu·was born alone, without a sister. Third, Damascius regards Enlil as an offspring of Anshar and Kishar, whereas the cuneiform record does not give Enlil's ancestry. Damascius probably derived this information from some other cuneiform source, for it is correct. Fourth, Damascius says that he conceives Mummu to be "the mental world," that is, the world as it exists in the mind of the creator before it becomes an external reality. This interpretation may have been suggested to Damascius by Plato's conception of the *logos.* Finally, it is not without interest that Damascius places the names of the goddesses before those of the gods, thus reversing the order in *Enûma elish.*

[78] A variant has *Mumis,* which is obviously the better reading.

[79] Charles E. Ruelle, Δαμασκίου διαδόχου ἀπορίαι καὶ λύσεις περὶ τῶν πρώτων ἀρχῶν (Paris, 1889), Part I, pp. 321 f.

[80] Cf. *Enûmu elish,* Tablet III:125.

The other Greek account is that of Berossus, a priest of Bêl Marduk at Babylon. It is taken from his history of Babylonia, which he compiled from native documents and published in Greek about 275 B.C.[81] His writings have perished, but extracts from his history have fortunately been preserved to us. The preservation of the excerpt dealing with his version of the Babylonian creation story we owe to a monk in Constantinople commonly known as Syncellus, or Synkellos (eighth century A.D.),[82] who derived this material from the lost *Chronicle* of the church historian Eusebius of Caesarea (*ca.* A.D. 260–*ca.* 340); and Eusebius, in turn, derived it from the works of Alexander Polyhistor (last century B.C.).[83] This account reads as follows:

He says there was a time in which all was darkness and water, wherein strange and peculiarly shaped creatures came into being; that there were born men with two wings, some also with four wings and two faces; (some) also having one body but two heads, the one of a man, the other of a woman, being likewise in their genitals both male and female; and that there were other human beings with legs and horns of goats; that some had horses' feet; that others had the limbs of a horse behind, but before were fashioned like men, resembling hippocentaurs; that, likewise, bulls with the heads of men bred there; and dogs with fourfold bodies and the tails of fish; also horses with the heads of dogs; and men and other creatures with the heads and bodies of horses and the tails of fishes; and other creatures with the shapes of every species of animals; that besides these there were fishes, and reptiles, and serpents, and still other wondrous creatures, which had appearances derived from one another; that of these are set up images in the temple of Bēl; (and) that over all these (creatures) ruled a woman named Omorka.[84] This in Chaldean is *thamte*,[85] meaning in Greek "the sea," but in numerical value it is equal to "moon."[86]

He says that all things being in this condition, Bēl came and clove the woman in two; and that out of one half of her he formed the earth, but with

[81] On this date see C. F. Lehmann-Haupt in *Reallexikon der Assyriologie*, II, 2–3.

[82] See Pauly-Wissowa, *Real-Encyclopädie der classischen Altertumswissenschaft*, 2. Reihe, Vol. VIII (Stuttgart, 1932), cols. 1388 ff.

[83] *Encyclopaedia Britannica* (14th ed.; London and New York, 1929), III, 460.

[84] *Omorka* (an emendation for *Omórōka*) is a title of Tiʾâmat.

[85] The Greek text has *thalatth*, which is obviously a scribal error (see W. Robertson Smith in *Zeitschrift für Assyriologie*, VI [1891], 339). The form *thamte* corresponds to the Babylonian *tâmtu*, denoting the sea, the ocean, or Tiʾâmat (the personified primordial sea, or ocean).

[86] I.e., 'Ομόρκα (Omorka) and σελήνη ("moon") have the same numerical value, viz., 301.

the other half the sky; and that he destroyed the creatures within her; but that this was an allegorical description of nature; for while the whole universe consisted of moisture and such living creatures had been born therein, Bēl, who is identified with Zeus, divided the darkness in two, separated heaven and earth from one another, and reduced the universe to order; but that the living things, not being able to bear the strength of the light, perished; that this Bēl, upon perceiving that the land was desolate and bearing no fruit,[87] commanded one of the gods to cut off his head,[88] (that he also commanded the other gods) to mix the blood which flowed forth with earth, and to form men and animals capable of bearing the air; that this Bēl also formed the stars, the sun, the moon, and the five planets. These things,[89] according to Alexander Polyhistor, Berossus told in his first book: that this god cut off his own head, and that the other gods mixed the blood which flowed forth with earth and formed men; that on this account they are rational and partake of divine understanding.[90]

This version again accords with *Enûma elish* to a remarkable degree, deviating from it and Damascius in only a few details. We notice at once that, while Damascius deals almost exclusively with the origin of the gods, Berossus passes that subject over in silence but presupposes the existence of the gods in the second part of his narrative. Considering, however, what a detailed account he gives us of the monsters that dwelt in the deep at the time when "all was darkness and water," we may perhaps assume that this omission is due not to Berossus but to Alexander Polyhistor, to whom we owe this extract and who was perhaps more interested in the strange creatures that existed before heaven and earth had been formed than in the theogonic views of the Babylonians.[91]

The fabulous beings with which the account of Berossus is largely concerned represent, of course, the monsters which

---

[87] To be emended thus for the Greek "fruit-bearing," which is due to a slight error; the scribe wrote καρποφόρον instead of ἀκαρποφόρον.

[88] I.e., this god (the Kingu of the cuneiform story), upon Bêl Marduk's command, should cut off his own head, not Marduk's head, as is frequently held (cf. *Enûma elish*, Tablet VI: 1–33).

[89] From here on we have the words of Eusebius.

[90] *Eusebi chronicorum libri duo*, ed. Alfred Schoene, Vol. I (Berlin, 1875), cols. 14–18. In the second paragraph I follow the text as it has been transposed by Alfred von Gutschmid, cited *ibid.*, col. 16, n. 9.

[91] Cf. P. Schnabel, *Berossos und die babylonisch-hellenistische Literatur* (Leipzig and Berlin, 1923), pp. 138 and 177.

Ti°âmat created to aid her in the warfare against the gods (*Enûma elish*, Tablet I:132–45). But Berossus' description of them, as it has come down to us, bears only a general resemblance to the cuneiform narrative and is probably based on the "images" which were "set up in the temple of Bēl" rather than on the Babylonian creation story itself.

Berossus says that "there was a time in which all was darkness and water." The "water" he subsequently identifies with "a woman named Omorka," who, he says, "in Chaldean [i.e., Babylonian] is *thamte*, meaning in Greek 'the sea.' " Then in the following paragraph he calls this same woman "darkness." In other words, the "darkness and water" of which Berossus speaks at the beginning of his account is the Ti°âmat of the cuneiform original; it is the personification of the primordial salt-water ocean enveloped in darkness.

Of great interest also is the allegorical interpretation which Berossus puts on the conflict between Marduk and Ti°âmat and the subsequent creation of heaven and earth with the carcass of Ti°âmat. Here Berossus is obviously making a concession to certain Greek philosophers in order to render Babylonian speculation more acceptable to them, without implying, however, that he came upon this kind of interpretation through the study of Greek thought. On the contrary, the type of interpretation which Berossus here follows was doubtless known to all thinkers of Babylonia and Assyria. Every priest knew that Ti°âmat was nothing but the dark primeval salt-water ocean personified, containing all the elements of which heaven and earth were afterward made, for up to the latest times of Babylonian-Assyrian history *tâmtu* (a later development of *ti°âmatu*, which when applied to the primeval female principle was shortened to *ti°âmat*) was used as the regular designation for the sea or ocean.[92]

According to *Enûma elish*, Tablet VI, the creation of man was motivated by the fact that the gods were in need of worshipers who would build and maintain their temples and who would bring offerings and sacrifices to them for the purpose of supplying their wants. Berossus, on the other hand, attributes

[92] For the view presented in this paragraph see *ibid.*, p. 178.

this act of Marduk to the desolate and unproductive condition
of the land. This is, of course, not a conflicting but rather a
supplementary element in the account of Berossus; man was
created because the gods needed someone who would, among
other things, till the soil and make it produce fruit for their
sustenance. The source from which Berossus derived this idea
may have been the story which in this volume bears the title
"Another Account of the Creation of Man" (pp. 68–71).

Berossus states that man was formed from the blood of a god
mixed with earth, whereas *Enûma elish*, Tablet VI:33, mentions only blood as the substance from which man was fashioned
and does not refer to the mixing of the blood with earth. The
point expressed by Berossus was probably understood in the
cuneiform passage under consideration, for if man had been
formed solely with the blood of Kingu, he would be all divine,
he would be just another god, although of very low degree.
Nevertheless, it seems reasonable to surmise that also here
Berossus drew upon another version of the way in which man
came into being. He may have based his remark on the account
entitled "The Creation of Man" (pp. 66–67), according to which
a god was slain and his flesh and blood were then mixed with
earth to make man.

Furthermore, Berossus says that animals as well as men were
created from divine blood which had been mixed with earth,
whereas Tablet VI of *Enûma elish* states only that *man* was
formed with divine blood. The creation of animals is not mentioned at all in *Enûma elish*. However, since men and animals,
according to Berossus, were fashioned with the blood of one and
the same god, and since in *Enûma elish* the killing of a god for
the purpose of creating other beings is first conceived and executed on Tablet VI, we might expect that the creation of animals was recorded somewhere on Tablet VI, after that of man.
But there is no room for that anywhere. It is therefore possible
that here Berossus bases his narrative on another creation
legend, according to which animals as well as men were created
from divine blood, or that Polyhistor or Eusebius made a mistake in summarizing the account of Berossus, and that Berossus
never attributed a common origin to human beings and ani-

mals. For if the animals share the same origin with men, should they not also be "rational and partake of divine understanding"?

Finally, according to Berossus, the god from whose blood men and animals were formed cut off his own head. Here Berossus again deviates from the main creation account, according to which certain gods "inflicted punishment" on Kingu "by cutting (the arteries of) his blood" (Tablet VI:32). There is no cuneiform source to support Berossus on this point.

There can be no doubt not only that Berossus based his account on *Enûma elish* but that he utilized a number of different Babylonian creation stories. Moreover, it is not unreasonable to assume that his account has not been epitomized correctly in all details. Nevertheless, even in the condition in which it has been transmitted to us, it is an interesting and valuable piece of literature.

CHAPTER III

OLD TESTAMENT PARALLELS

SCHOLARS all over the world have long recognized that the Babylonian accounts presented in translation on the preceding pages contain a considerable number of points which invite comparison not only with the first few chapters of the Book of Genesis but also with various other portions of the Old Testament. Thus *Enûma elish* and Gen. 1:1—2:3 both refer to a watery chaos, which was separated into heaven and earth; in both we have an etymological equivalence in the names denoting this chaos; both refer to the existence of light before the creation of the luminous bodies; both agree as to the succession in which the points of contact follow upon one another; and in both cases the number seven figures rather prominently. And turning to the poetic writings of our Old Testament literature, we find quite a number of passages which, like the story of Marduk's fight with Tiʾâmat, treat of a conflict between the Creator and various hostile elements.

These and other parallels between the Babylonian cosmological texts and the Old Testament have led many scholars to the conclusion that the biblical passages in question are founded upon Babylonian exemplars. It is the purpose of this chapter to determine whether this view can be maintained, and, should it be found correct, it will be the further purpose to inquire into the extent to which the Old Testament passages in question are dependent on Babylonian sources and what implications this may then have for questions of religious faith. To this end we shall examine all the more outstanding points of comparison between Babylonian cosmology and the Old Testament, consider the main arguments that can be advanced pro and con, and draw our conclusions. Chief among these points of comparison are the following.

DIVINE PRINCIPLES

The Babylonians and Assyrians assumed two sexually distinct divine principles, called Apsû and Tiʾâmat, the former being masculine and the latter feminine. Apsû was the father of the gods and Tiʾâmat the mother. Tiʾâmat is almost universally held to have been a dragon or some serpentine monster of a forbidding aspect. Since this point will become of importance later on in this chapter, it will be advisable to consider it in some detail.

The evidence which has been cited in support of the view that Tiʾâmat was a dragon is taken chiefly from Babylonian and Assyrian art and literature. The literary evidence is based principally on a few passages in *Enûma elish* and on a story which in this volume bears the title "The Slaying of the *Labbu*" (see Appendix).

It has been urged that since *Enûma elish* (Tablet I: 132 ff.) represents Tiʾâmat as having borne monster-serpents, Tiʾâmat must herself have been a great and powerful serpent, or some serpent-like monster.[1] Against this, however, it must be remembered that Tiʾâmat gave birth also to the good and benevolent gods, who expressly call her "our bearer" (Tablets II: 11 and III: 15), and that, even after she has brought forth monsters, Marduk still calls her "a woman" (Tablet II: 110 f.),[2] as does also Berossus. Tiʾâmat was a goddess, and as such she could give birth to dragons without herself being a dragon.

The second passage from *Enûma elish* which has been quoted in this connection is found on Tablet IV: 97, which states that "Tiʾâmat opened her mouth to *devour*" Marduk as he approached her in deadly combat.[3] But this does not necessarily

---

[1] Thus Friedrich Delitzsch, *Babel and Bible* (trans. from the German; Chicago, 1906), p. 159.

[2] Thᵒ assertion made by L. W. King, *The Seven Tablets of Creation* (London, 1902) , lxxi, n. 1, that the term "woman" is employed with reference to Tiʾâmat's sex and not to her form cannot be maintained. The natural interpretation of Tablet II: 110 f. quite obviously is that Marduk, in his statement to Anshar, regards Tiʾâmat as one of their own kind. H. Gunkel's idea (*Genesis* [Göttingen, 1917], p. 126), that Tiʾâmat was originally a female monster which in later times was conceived as a woman, is groundless.

[3] King, *loc. cit.*

make Ti°âmat a dragon. For analogous cases we may point to
the Greek god Kronos, who swallowed almost all his children,
and to Polyphemus, the one-eyed Cyclops who imprisoned
Odysseus (or Ulysses) and devoured several of the latter's com-
panions. No one would call them dragons. Ti°âmat was such a
gigantic being that she felt she could swallow up Marduk; and
since under the circumstances this may have appeared to her to
be the most expeditious way of getting rid of Marduk, or even
the only way of salvation, she tried to do it.

The third of the more important passages that have been in-
voked are two broken lines in the story "The Slaying of the
Labbu." Lines 5 and 6 of this myth have been translated by
King[4] and others as follows:

> Who was the dragon [. . . .]?
> Ti°âmat was the dragon [. . . .].

In more recent years, however, a tablet has been found at
Ashur which contains another version of "The Slaying of the
Labbu" and which shows beyond doubt that the above lines
must be restored and translated about as follows:

> Who [brought forth] the serpent(-dragon)?
> The sea [brought forth] the serpent(-dragon).

This, of course, invalidates the argument completely. Furthermore, the monster of which this legend speaks appeared *after* the
creation of the universe, after the earth had already been popu-
lated by man, and therefore it cannot be identical with Ti°âmat,
out of whose body Marduk fashioned heaven and earth. Finally,
in this myth the dragon is masculine, as is evidenced by the
verbs and suffixes referring to it, while Ti°âmat was feminine.[5]

---

[4] *Ibid.*, pp. 116 f.

[5] The assertion by Erich Ebeling, *Tod und Leben nach den Vorstellungen der
Babylonier* (Berlin and Leipzig, 1931), p. 35, that Ti°âmat was bisexual is ill-found-
ed. The text to which Ebeling refers is a late astrological-mythological commentary
dating from about the period of the Arsacidae. The passage in question reads: "The
mouth-star = the corpse-star; its name is Ti°âmat the she-ibex(?); *it* has two
faces, *it* is male and female." The text states in unequivocal terms that the
"mouth-star" is male and female. While it is difficult to determine the exact meaning of this line, there is no warrant for the deduction that Ti°âmat herself, the
mother of the gods, was conceived as being both male and female.

To this category belong two texts which to my knowledge have not yet been quoted in proof of the dragon-like appearance of Tiʾâmat but which may lead one to such a conclusion. The first text is a late commentary to certain rituals, particularly of the New Year's festival, and has been published by Erich Ebeling in *Keilschrifttexte aus Assur religiösen Inhalts*, No. 307. The lines which concern us at the moment are found on the reverse of the tablet and read as follows:

1. "... Tiʾâmat, the lord vanquished [her],
2. [He sei]zed her, decreed her destiny, and split her open like a mussel(?) into two (parts).
3. Her two right eyes are the Tigris, her two left eyes are the Euphrates.
11. The wild ass is the departed spirit of Enlil; the jackal is the departed spirit of Anu.
13. The camel is the departed spirit of Tiʾâmat; the lord cut off her horns.
14. He severed her [ho]rns (and) cut off her tail."[6]

This quotation elucidates the second text to which I have just referred. It is a small and very fragmentary Neo-Babylonian commentary to *Enûma elish* and has been published by King (*The Seven Tablets of Creation*, Vol. II, Pl. LXII [R. 395]). The two lines in question read:

> Out of her eyes he opened the river[s Tigris and Euphrates].
> He twisted (*e-gir*) her tail into a *durma[ḫu*(?). ...].

Considering that this passage is taken from a commentary to *Enûma elish* and considering the very similar phraseology in the text quoted a moment ago, it is obvious that "her tail" has reference to the tail of Tiʾâmat.

According to these later materials, Tiʾâmat had not only four eyes, like Marduk, but also horns and a tail. The last two characteristics may seem to justify or even necessitate the conclusion that we are here dealing with a dragon-like monster. However, the horns may possibly refer to the horns of the divine tiara, which in later times were "the invariable mark of a divini-

---

[6] For a transliteration and a translation of this text see Ebeling, *Tod und Leben.* ... , pp. 31–37. Cf. also Benno Landsberger in *Archiv für Keilschriftforschung*, I (Neudruck, 1938), 46, n. 6. This "Neudruck" (or second printing) contains a valuable additional note.

ty,"[7] while the idea of a tail may have been suggested by the fact that the departed spirit of Tiᵓâmat was visualized as a camel, just as the departed spirits of Enlil and Anu were pictured as the wild ass and the jackal, respectively. On the other hand, it is at least equally possible that Tiᵓâmat, like Ishtar, Ningal, Ninlil, and Ninsun,[8] was portrayed or conceived also as a wild cow. At any rate, the horns and the tail show as little that Tiᵓâmat was a dragon as the same features prove the dragon-like nature of the bull-man, represented in glyptic art.[9]

The second type of evidence adduced in support of the contention that Tiᵓâmat was a dragon, or some such creature, is derived from Babylonian and Assyrian sculpture and cylinder seals.[10]

Perhaps the most important of these pictorial representations is found on two slabs coming from the entrance to the temple of the warrior-god Ninurta at Nimrûd (the biblical Calah).[11] The two slabs are sculptured and picture a winged god with two thunderbolts in pursuit of a monster which is half-lion and half-bird. Across the picture runs an inscription starting with an invocation to Ninurta (Figs. 6 and 7).[12] In certain quarters this picture is still believed to portray the fight between Marduk and Tiᵓâmat. But since the inscription begins with a prayer to Ninurta and since the sculpture comes from one of his temples, there can be no doubt that the deity pursuing the monster is Ninurta and not Marduk. As for the monster, it is clearly masculine, whereas Tiᵓâmat was feminine. Moreover, it is a creature of the land and the air, while Tiᵓâmat was a water deity. The

---

[7] E. Douglas van Buren in *Archiv für Orientforschung*, X (1935/36), 59. Such horns were worn also by goddesses (see H. Frankfort, *Cylinder Seals* [London, 1939], pp. 22 and 32).

[8] Knut Tallqvist, *Akkadische Götterepitheta* (Helsinki, 1938), p. 166.

[9] See Frankfort, *op. cit.*, pp. 61 and 171.

[10] See. W. H. Ward, *The Seal Cylinders of Western Asia* (Washington, D.C., 1910), pp. 197–212.

[11] E. A. Wallis Budge, *Assyrian Sculptures in the British Museum, Reign of Ashur-nasir-pal* (London, 1914), Pl. XXXVII; C. J. Gadd, *The Stones of Assyria* (London, 1936), p. 138, Nos. 27–29.

[12] For a translation of the inscription see Budge and King, *Annals of the Kings of Assyria* (London, 1902), pp. 254 ff.

theory is further weakened by the fact that on a plaster impression of a cylinder seal in the Walters Art Gallery (Baltimore) the same dragon is attacked by a winged god or semigod with scorpioid attributes,[13] showing that also in this case the aggressive deity is not Marduk.

The beast which in Figure 1 is resting at the feet of Marduk has also been identified with Tiʾâmat.[14] In its fully developed form it is a composite monster, with the elongated head, the forked tongue, and scale-covered body of a serpent; with the forelegs of a lion and the hind legs of an eagle or some such bird; and with an upright horn and a wriggling tail, terminating in the sting of a scorpion (Fig. 5). But it should be observed that the Marduk statue (Fig. 1) represents the monster merely as *subdued*, at the most, while Tiʾâmat was *slain* and her body split in two and used in the creation of heaven and earth. Furthermore, it can be stated with almost complete certainty that this composite being is the same as the dragon mentioned in Tablet I:140.[15] There, however, we learn that the dragon was not Tiʾâmat herself but one of the creatures brought forth by her. There is no reason whatever why this monster should be identified with Tiʾâmat.

Of the cylinder seals mentioned in connection with this subject, perhaps the most interesting is the one on which appears a huge horned serpent with two short arms and two hands, pursued by a god armed with thunderbolts in each hand (Fig. 8). But neither here nor in any other instance is the name of Tiʾâmat found in connection with the pictorial rendition. Identification of this or any other Babylonian or Assyrian monster with Tiʾâmat is without any factual basis; this could be done only if we had literary evidence to warrant it.

[13] See Cyrus H. Gordon in *Iraq*, VI (1939), Pl. XI, Fig. 88 (cf. also E. Unger's treatment of the scorpion-man in *Reallexikon der Vorgeschichte*, VIII [1927], 201–2). Another close parallel to the pictorial rendering from Nimrûd has been published by E. Douglas van Buren in *Orientalia*, XV (New ser., 1946), Pl. VIII, Fig. 32 (discussed *ibid.*, pp. 40–42).

[14] Delitzsch, *op. cit.*, p. 159, and Unger, *Babylon, die heilige Stadt* (Berlin and Leipzig, 1931), p. 210.

[15] See H. Zimmern in E. Schrader, *Die Keilinschriften und das Alte Testament* (Berlin, 1903), p. 504.

In general, it should be remembered that dragons were most likely much more numerous in Babylonian and Assyrian religious belief than the available cuneiform records would indicate. Thus we find that the number of monsters mentioned by Berossus in his description of conditions prior to the formation of heaven and earth far exceeds the list given in Enûma elish, but, according to H. Frankfort,[16] all these figures are known from the seals. It would therefore be a mistake if we tried to identify every dragon portrayed in Babylonian or Assyrian art with some dreadful monster referred to in the inscriptions.[17]

No conclusive proof has yet been found for the idea that Tiɔâmat was a dragon, or a similar being, while against it can be cited the testimony of Berossus and of Enûma elish to the effect that Tiɔâmat was a woman, the wife of Apsû, and the mother of the gods. Jensen[18] is therefore unquestionably right in his declaration that the supposed dragon-form of Tiɔâmat is "a pure figment of the imagination" (ein reines Phantasiegebilde).[19]

Apsû and Tiɔâmat were not simply the ancestors of the gods. They represented at the same time the living, uncreated worldmatter; Apsû was the primeval sweet-water ocean, and Tiɔâmat the primeval salt-water ocean.[20] They were matter and divine spirit united and coexistent, like body and soul. In them were contained all the elements of which the universe was made later on, and from them were descended all the gods and goddesses of the vast Babylonian-Assyrian pantheon.

[16] Op. cit., p. 199.

[17] For further information on the dragon in ancient Mesopotamia see Unger in Reallexikon der Vorgeschichte, VIII, 195–216, and E. Douglas van Buren in Orientalia, XV, 1–45, where many additional references will be found. On the "monster" Kur, which S. N. Kramer, Sumerian Mythology (Philadelphia, 1944), pp. 76–96, thought to have detected, see T. Jacobsen in the Journal of Near Eastern Studies, V (1946), 143–47.

[18] In Reallexikon der Assyriologie, II, 85 (under "Chaos").

[19] Cf. also Jensen, Das Gilgamesch-Epos in der Weltliteratur, I (Strassburg, 1906), 60–63. The same view has been expressed by Witton Davies in his discussion of the apocryphal story of Bel and the Dragon (see R. H. Charles, The Apocrypha and Pseudepigrapha of the Old Testament [Oxford, 1913], I, 653 f.).

[20] Jensen in Reallexikon der Assyriologie, I, 122–24; A. Deimel, "Enuma Eliš" und Hexaëmeron (Rome, 1934), p. 22.

In sharp contrast to this, the Book of Genesis speaks of only one divine principle, existing apart from and independently of all cosmic matter.

WHENCE MATTER?

From what has just been said relative to the nature of Apsû and Tiʾâmat it is apparent that for the Babylonians matter was eternal. This conclusion is confirmed by the historian Diodorus Siculus (last century B.c.), who expressly states: "The Chaldeans say that the substance (φύσις) of the world is eternal (ἀΐδιος) and that it neither had a first beginning nor that it will at a later time suffer destruction."[21] The Babylonians could conceive of a time when there was neither heaven nor earth, a time when only Apsû and Tiʾâmat existed, but apparently they could not conceive of a time when there was nothing whatever except a transcendental deity; they postulated the existence of the material as well as that of the spiritual or the divine.

Genesis, chapter 1, on the other hand, predicates a creation out of nothing (*creatio ex nihilo*), that is to say, it asserts that by the sovereign will and power of God matter was brought into existence from vacuous nothing at the creation of the universe.[22]

This concept, however, cannot be deduced from the Hebrew verb *bārâ*, "to create," as it has been done. For although this term is invariably employed to designate the creative activities of God and "never takes the accusative of the material from which a thing is made, as do other verbs of making, but uses the accusative to designate only the thing made,"[23] there is no conclusive evidence in the entire Old Testament that the verb itself ever expresses the idea of a creation out of nothing. This applies even to Gen. 2:3b, which is probably best rendered as follows: "For on it He rested from all His work, in doing which God had

[21] ii.30. On the above translation of φύσις see H. G. Liddell and R. Scott, *A Greek-English Lexicon*, revised and augmented by Sir Henry Stuart Jones, Part 10 (Oxford, 1940), p. 1965.

[22] This is not identical with the Vedic concept of creation out of a seeming or transcendental nothing (i.e., a transcendental substance originating in and emanating from the deity), on which see Carl A. Scharbau, *Die Idee der Schöpfung in der Vedischen Literatur* (Stuttgart, 1932), esp. pp. 33–35 and 72–82.

[23] Julian Morgenstern in the *American Journal of Semitic Languages and Literatures*, XXXVI (1920), 201.

brought about creation."[24] *Bārâ* occurs as a synonym of *ʿāśâ*, "to do," "to make" (Gen. 1:21-27; 5:2; Isa. 41:20; 43:7); *yāṣar*, "to form," "to fashion" (Isa. 43:1 and 7; 45:7 and 18; Amos 4:13); *kônēn* (the *pôlēl* of *kûn*), "to set up," "to establish" (Isa. 45:18); and of *yāsad*, "to found" (Ps. 89:12 f.). The Septuagint usually renders *bārâ* by ποιεῖν ("to do," "to make") or κτίζειν ("to found," "to create"), but never by ποιεῖν ἐξ οὐκ ὄντων ("to make out of nothing"), or the like. In South Arabic the root *brʾ* signifies "to make," "to construct."[25] Hebrew *bārâ* has about the same meaning as *ʿāśâ*, with this difference, that *bārâ* contains the idea of a new[26] and extraordinary or epochal production, never necessitating toil on the part of the Creator,[27] while *ʿāśâ* is used in the general, colorless sense of "to do" or "to make." But the idea of a creation out of nothing is a connotation which has been read into *bārâ;*[28] the same applies to Latin *creare,*[29] from which, of course, the English verb "to create" is derived, and to the German *schaffen.*[30]

However, the doctrine in question *can* be deduced from the expression *běrêshîth*, "in the beginning" (Gen. 1:1), i.e., in the very beginning of things (cf. ἐν ἀρχῇ in John 1:1). At *that time* God created "heaven and earth." Elsewhere in the Old Testament the phrase "heaven and earth" denotes the *organized*

[24] Cf. T. J. Meek in J. M. P. Smith and Edgar J. Goodspeed, *The Bible: An American Translation* (Chicago, 1935). For the grammatical construction see *Gesenius' Hebrew Grammar*, edited and enlarged by E. Kautzsch and translated by A. E. Cowley (Oxford, 1910), sec. 114, *o;* and Franz Delitzsch, *Neuer Commentar über die Genesis* (Leipzig, 1887), p. 70 (esp. Eccles. 2:11).

[25] See Karolus Conti Rossini, *Chrestomathia Arabica Meridionalis Epigraphica* (Rome, 1931), p. 117.

[26] In Isa. 41:20; 43:1 and 15; 65:18; Pss. 51:12; 102:19; 104:30 it is used in the sense of re-creating something, of creating something new but with old material.

[27] However, not always merely by word or volition; for sometimes additional means are obviously employed (cf., e.g., Isa. 43:7; 54:16; Mal. 2:10).

[28] For a detailed discussion of *bārâ* see Franz Böhl's article in *Alttestamentliche Studien Rudolf Kittel . . . . dargebracht* (Leipzig, 1913), pp. 42-60.

[29] In ecclesiastical Latin *creare* does have the idea of a creation out of nothing but not in classical Latin (see A. Ernout and A. Millet, *Dictionnaire étymologique de la langue latine* [Paris, 1939], p. 230).

[30] Friedrich Kluge, *Etymologisches Wörterbuch der deutschen Sprache* (Berlin and Leipzig, 1934), p. 504.

heaven and earth, the *organized* universe, the cosmos. This alone, however, does not prove that it must of necessity have the same meaning in the opening verse of Genesis, which introduces the account of how heaven and earth were created and organized. Elsewhere also the word "earth" denotes the *organized* earth, but in Gen. 1:2 it undeniably refers to the earth "in its primitive chaotic, unformed state."[31] This usage clearly decides the signification of "earth" in the preceding verse; and that, in turn, determines the sense in which "heaven" is to be taken in the same verse. This fact and the circumstance that the following verses describe the elaboration and completion of heaven and earth[32] justify us in concluding that in the initial verse of Genesis the phrase under discussion designates heaven and earth as first created out of nothing in a rude state but in their essential or basic form.[33]

This interpretation is completely in line with the following passages: "The Lord formed me[34] as the beginning of His way(s),[35] as the first of His works of old; from everlasting was I established, from the beginning, from the origin of the earth; when there were no depths was I brought into being, when there were no fountains heavy-laden with water; when He had not yet made the earth and the fields, nor the first of the clods of the world" (Prov. 8:22–26); "I beseech thee, O child, lift thine eyes to heaven and earth, look at all that is therein, and know that God did not make them out of things that existed" (ὅτι οὐκ ἐξ ὄντων ἐποίησεν αὐτὰ ὁ θεός [II Macc. 7:28]);[36] "In the beginning was the Word, and the Word was with God, and the Word was God. The same was with God in the beginning. All things were made through Him, and without Him not one thing was made that is made" (John 1:1–3); "By faith we perceive

[31] S. R. Driver, *The Book of Genesis* (London, 1904), p. 3.

[32] For the elaboration of the celestial regions see vss. 6–8 and 14–19.

[33] A *creatio ex nihilo* has been derived from Gen. 1:1 also by J. Wellhausen, *Prolegomena zur Geschichte Israels* (Berlin and Leipzig, 1927), p. 296, and W. Eichrodt, *Theologie des Alten Testaments*, II (Leipzig, 1935), 50 f.

[34] I.e., Wisdom.

[35] I.e., procedure, performance, or creation (cf. Job 26:14; 40:19).

[36] Alfred Rahlfs, *Septuaginta* (Stuttgart, 1935), I, 1117.

that the universe was created by the word of God, so that the things which are seen were not made of things which appear" (Heb. 11:3). There is not a single passage in the entire Bible which teaches the opposite.

This interpretation, however, has been seriously contested. For some commentators, either leaving *bārâ* (בָּרָא) intact[37] or changing it to the infinitive construct, *běrô* (בְּרֹא), hold that the initial verse of Genesis forms a subordinate clause and that the second verse predicates a pre-existent chaos. Some therefore translate the introductory verses of Genesis as follows: "When God began to create heaven and earth—the earth being a desolate waste, with darkness upon the abyss and the spirit of God hovering over the waters—God said: 'Let there be light!' And there was light." Others translate: "When God began to create heaven and earth, the earth was a desolate waste and darkness was upon the abyss and the spirit of God hovered over the waters. And God said: 'Let there be light!' And there was light." This view is based chiefly on the twofold assumption that *běrêshîth*, because of the lack of the definite article, stands in the construct state and that Gen. 1:2 would have to begin with *wattěhî hāʾāreṣ* (instead of *wě-hāʾāreṣ hāyěthā*) if verse 1 were an independent sentence.[38]

But terms like *rêshîth*, "beginning,"[39] *rôsh*, "beginning,"[40] *qedem*, "olden times," and *ʿôlām*, "eternity," when used in adverbial expressions, occur almost invariably *without* the article, and that in the absolute state.[41] In the Greek transliterations of

[37] On this construction see *Gesenius' Hebrew Grammar*, sec. 130, *d*.

[38] Thus Schrader, *Studien zur Kritik und Erklärung der biblischen Urgeschichte* (Zurich, 1863), pp. 43–47; and, less emphatically, J. M. P. Smith in the *American Journal of Semitic Languages and Literatures*, XLIV (1927/28), 108–10.

[39] For which cf. esp. Isa. 46:10, which has *mêrêshîth* in place of *min-hārêshîth* or *mêhārêshîth*.

[40] Cf. *mêrôsh*, Isa. 40:21; 41:4; Prov. 8:23; Eccles. 3:11.

[41] See Eduard König, *Historisch-comparative Syntax der hebräischen Sprache* (Leipzig, 1897), sec. 294, *g*, and *Die Genesis* (Gütersloh, 1919), p. 130, n. 1. W. F. Albright, in the *Journal of Biblical Literature*, LXII (1943), 369–70, denies the validity of this argument on the grounds that *mêʿôlām* and *miqqedem* are "old expressions probably going back to the age preceding the introduction of the article into common use in Hebrew" and that *mêrôsh* and *mêrêshîth* "occur only in verse, where the article is not nearly so frequent as in prose, owing to the conservative

the Hebrew text which have come down to us, *bĕrêshîth* in the opening verse of Genesis appears as βαρησήθ, βαρησέθ, βρησίθ, βρισήθ, and βρησίδ; Jerome transliterated it *bresith*.[42] This may be simply an indication that instead of *bĕrêshîth* (בְּרֵאשִׁית), which we should normally expect on the basis of the usage of this and similar Hebrew words, one could also say *bârêshîth* (בָּרֵאשִׁית), without any difference in meaning. The transliterations βαρησήθ and βαρησέθ support the old and generally accepted translation and interpretation of verse 1, while the absence of the definite article in *bĕrêshîth* cannot be used as a point against it.

The second argument, viz., that verse 2 would have to begin with *wattĕhî hā>āreṣ* if verse 1 really formed an independent statement, is equally untenable. The first verse of Genesis briefly records the creation of the universe in its essential form, and the second verse singles out a part of this universe, viz., the earth, and describes its condition in some detail. In verse 2 the emphasis thus rests on *earth*, and for this reason the subject is placed *before* the verb. For analogous examples we may quote the following lines: "And God called the light 'day,' but the darkness he called 'night'" (*wĕ-laḥōshek qārâ lāyĕlā*) (Gen. 1:5a); "Now the serpent was (*wĕ-hannāḥāsh hāyâ*) more clever than any beast of the field" (Gen. 3:1); *bānîm giddaltî wĕ-rômamtî wĕ-hēm pāshĕ<û bî*, "Sons have I reared and brought up, but they have rebelled against me!" (Isa. 1:2b). In the last passage, the two perfect forms *giddaltî* and *rômamtî* correspond to the perfect *bārâ* in Gen. 1:1, and the phrase *wĕ-hēm pāshĕ<û*

---

or archaistic character of poetry." Albright's first point, founded chiefly on conjecture, need not detain us. As regards his second point, it is to be noted that the introductory chapter of Genesis is not so prosaic as Albright's statement seems to indicate. In the very first two expressions we have alliteration (בָּרָא בְּרֵאשִׁית); in the second verse there is assonance (*tohû wābohû*); in verse 24 we meet the archaic construct *ḥayĕthô* followed by >*ereṣ* without the article (as against vs. 25); and verses 27–28 are poetry pure and simple. The whole chapter is written in a solemn tone and in dignified prose (cf. Gunkel, *op. cit.*, p. 117), which easily glides over into poetry.

42 Fridericus Field, *Origenis Hexaplorum quae supersunt*, Vol. I (Oxford, 1875), 7; Paul de Lagarde, *Ankündigung einer neuen Ausgabe der griechischen Uebersetzung des Alten Testaments* (Göttingen, 1882), p. 5.

corresponds to *wĕ-hāʾāreṣ hāyĕthā* in verse 2. The second verse
of the first chapter of Genesis could also be rendered by "Now
the earth on her part was a desolate waste, ..."[43] There is
thus no necessity for the use of the imperfect tense in this
verse.[44]

The translations which take verse 1 as a temporal clause
yield good sense, but they militate against all the ancient versions and the simplest and most natural interpretation of the
Massoretic text. If the Massoretes had regarded verse 1 as a
temporal clause subordinate to what follows, they would probably have used the more natural form *bĕrô* (בְּרֹא) in order to
avoid ambiguity. While the verdict of the versions and of the
Massoretes is by no means final, it nevertheless deserves our
careful consideration and should not be set aside without good
reasons. And in the present case no such reasons exist. Furthermore, the sentence structure in the first of the two translations
treating verse 1 as a subordinate clause is unnecessarily com-
plicated, although it cannot be denied that involved construc-
tions do occur in the Old Testament (cf. Num. 5:12–15 and
Josh. 3:14–16). And in the case of the second translation we
should ordinarily expect verse 2 to begin with *wattĕhî* if the
meaning of the passage in question really were as translated
(cf. Jer. 7:25). There is no exact analogy anywhere to support
this translation, not even in Gen. 2:4 f., since *bĕyôm ʿaśôth* is
there followed by the imperfect, instead of the perfect.[45]

In further support of the translations which regard verse 1 as
a subordinate clause, reference has been made also to the Wisdom of Solomon (11:17): "For Thine all-powerful hand, that
created the world out of formless matter (ἐξ ἀμόρφου ὕλης),[46]
lacked not means to send upon them a multitude of bears, or
fierce lions." The Wisdom of Solomon is a combination of Greek
and Hebrew thought, and the expression "formless matter," as
it stands, conveys a purely Greek philosophical conception. One

43 In contradistinction to this passage, Isa. 45:18 ("He did not create it a
desolation" [*tohû*]) treats not of the preliminary stages of the earth but of the final
result.

44 König, *Die Genesis*, pp. 135 f.

45 See *ibid.*, pp. 137 f.   46 Rahlfs, *op. cit.*, II, 361.

could, no doubt, interpret this passage to mean that God first created shapeless matter and then formed the universe with it. However, since the author's aim was to advance the strongest possible arguments for the omnipotence of God, and since a creation out of nothing would have been a much more convincing demonstration of God's sovereign power than would the mere arrangement and orderly disposition of matter, he would not have used a phrase which to his Greek readers would convey the idea that matter was eternal and that God merely molded it to his purpose, had he believed in a creation out of nothing. We may therefore conclude with certainty that the author of the Wisdom of Solomon did not accept this doctrine but that, under the influence of Greek philosophy, he posited a pre-existent chaotic material.[47] And since his belief was based on Greek speculation, this passage cannot serve as argument either pro or con.[48]

A final argument to be considered very briefly in this connection is derived from the fact that most Mesopotamian creation stories begin with a subordinate clause, starting with *enûma* in Babylonian and *ud-da* in Sumerian, both of which expressions mean "on the day that" or simply "when" and correspond to Hebrew *běyôm*. But if the writer of the first chapter of Genesis had patterned the initial verse after the style of the Sumerian-Babylonian cosmologists, it would be most extraordinary that instead of using the Hebrew equivalent *běyôm* he introduced the expression *běrêshîth*, which finds no parallel in the cosmogonies of Mesopotamia. Had the biblical writer adopted the style of the Sumerian-Babylonian mythographers and had he purposed to start out with a subordinate sentence, he would in all probability have begun with the normal and unequivocal phrase *běyôm*, which is precisely what we find in Gen. 2:4 and 5:1–2, the latter passage, like the present verse, being assigned to the Priestly narrative by modern scholarship (cf. also Ezek. 28:13).

---

[47] See Charles, *op. cit.*, I, 553.

[48] This is true also of the works of the Jewish philosopher Philo of Alexandria (born shortly before the Christian Era); not only was he under the sway of Greek philosophy but he does not even seem to have been strictly consistent on the point at issue (see *The Jewish Encyclopedia* [New York and London, 1907], IV, 338).

Hence the usage of *běrêshîth* is far from being "the most obvious and clear-cut illustration of ultimate dependence on Mesopotamia in the Old Testament account of the Creation."[49] In fact, it points in the opposite direction.

Still other commentators treat the initial verse of Genesis as a superscription summarizing the entire creative process recorded in chapters 1:2—2:3. But the use of the copula *wě* ("and") at the beginning of verse 2 speaks against it.[50] This copula, which is here followed by a noun occupying an emphatic position, as we have seen, cannot attach itself to a heading. Besides, verse 1 would be a peculiar superscription.

POLYTHEISM AND MONOTHEISM

The Babylonian creation stories are permeated with a crude polytheism. They speak not only of successive generations of gods and goddesses proceeding from Apsû and Tiʾâmat, with all of them in need of physical nourishment, since all consist of matter as well as of spirit, but they speak also of different creators. According to *Enûma elish*, Apsû and Tiʾâmat are the ancestors of all the Babylonian and Assyrian divinities. But these in turn personify various cosmic spaces and the different forces in nature. Consequently, Apsû and Tiʾâmat are not simply the parents of divine beings, without having anything to do with the work of creation; but, by giving birth to these deities, they have a direct share in the actual creation of the universe. The earliest stages of creation are thus ascribed to sexual congress. Then after war had broken out among the gods, Ea killed Apsû, and with his carcass he formed the subterranean sea, on which the earth rests. Finally, after a considerable portion of the universe had thus been created, Marduk, the chief creator, appeared on the scene. He is credited with the creation of heaven and earth, the luminary bodies, grain and legumes, and, together with Ea, he is said to have fashioned man.

Other accounts tell us that "the gods in their assembly" made the world and the living creatures therein (p. 64); that Anu, Enlil, Shamash, and Ea created the universe and, to-

[49] Albright in the *Journal of Biblical Literature*, LXII, 369.
[50] König, *Die Genesis*, p. 135.

gether with the Anunnaki, formed the first two human beings, Ulligarra and Zalgarra (pp. 68–71); that Anu made the heavens, and that Ea created various minor patron deities, the king, and mankind (pp. 65–66); that Anu, Enlil, and Enki (i.e., Ea) created the moon and the sun (pp. 73–74); that Marduk was assisted by the goddess Aruru in his work of creating mankind (p. 63); and, finally, that the goddess Mami (also called Ninḫursag) at the behest of Enki and other deities fashioned man from clay mixed with the blood of a slain god (pp. 66–67).

Against all this, the opening chapters of Genesis as well as the Old Testament in general refer to only one Creator and Maintainer of all things, one God who created and transcends all cosmic matter. In the entire Old Testament, there is not a trace of a theogony, such as we find, for example, in *Enûma elish* and in Hesiod. To this faith the Babylonians never attained.

PRIMEVAL CHAOS

Enûma elish and Genesis, chapter 1, both refer to a watery chaos, a feature which is found also in the cosmologies of the Egyptians[51] and Phoenicians[52] and in the Vedic literature.[53] *Enûma elish* conceives of this chaos as *living* matter and as being an integral part of the first two principles, Apsû and Tiᵊâmat, in whom all the elements of the future universe were commingled, while, according to Genesis, it is nothing but a mass of *inanimate* matter, which was afterward separated into the waters above and below, into dry land and ocean.

The concept of a primeval ocean at the very beginning of time has repeatedly been advanced as a strong argument for the Babylonian origin of the biblical account of creation. *Enûma elish*, it is asserted, is a nature myth symbolizing the change of seasons from winter to spring. The watery chaos, it is held, reflects the heavy winter rains, the overflow of the rivers, and the

---

[51] W. M. Flinders Petrie in *Encyclopaedia of Religion and Ethics*, ed. Hastings, IV, 144; H. Grapow in *Zeitschrift für ägyptische Sprache und Altertumskunde*, LXVII (1931), 34.

[52] John Skinner, *A Critical and Exegetical Commentary on Genesis* (New York, 1910), pp. 48–49.

[53] Scharbau, *op. cit.*, pp. 36–37 and 46–51.

disorder which they cause, when the land of Babylonia is inundated; while the parting of the water and the creation of heaven and earth represent the spring, when the clouds and the water vanish, when Marduk, the god of the spring sun, appears and creates life and order. With this picture the biblical narrative is said to agree so closely that its importation from Babylonia to Palestine may be regarded as a certainty, especially if one considers how impossible it would have been for such an idea to arise on Hebrew soil, where climatic conditions are so much different.[54]

Some years ago, however, Albert T. Clay[55] called attention to the fact that the rainy season and the overflow of the rivers of Babylonia do not synchronize, and the average fall of rain in Babylonia, amounting to about six inches per year,[56] is too small to be of any consequence; in fact, it is so small that the land would be a desert were it not for the irrigation canals and the inundations. The rivers do not flood in the winter but in the spring, from March to June, following the melting of the snows on the Zagros and the mountains of Armenia. The watery chaos, resulting from the overflow of the rivers, sets in after the winter is over and after the god of the spring sun has made his appearance.

TIʾÂMAT AND TĔHÔM

In both accounts we find an etymological equivalence in the names by which this watery mass is designated. In *Enûma elish* it is the word *Tiʾâmat*, in Genesis the term *tĕhôm*, which occurs in 1:2 and is usually translated with "the deep." *Tiʾâmat* is almost invariably employed as a proper name; but rarely does it stand for *tâmtu*, a generic term for "ocean," "sea," or "lake." And the absence of the definite article in *tĕhôm*, with the exception of the plural forms in Ps. 106:9 and Isa. 63:13, shows that

[54] See Zimmern in *Der alte Orient*, II, Heft 3 (1903), 17; Driver, *op. cit.*, p. 28; and Jastrow in the *Journal of the American Oriental Society*, XXXVI (1917), 277 and 296.

[55] *The Origin of Biblical Traditions* (New Haven, Conn., 1923), pp. 75–78. See also George A. Barton's remarks in the *Journal of the American Oriental Society*, XLV (1925), 27 f., and Clay's rejoinder, *ibid.*, p. 141.

[56] See M. G. Ionides, *The Régime of the Rivers Euphrates and Tigris* (London and New York, 1937), esp. pp. 24–36.

tĕhôm comes close to being a proper name, corresponding in this respect to Hebrew *tēbēl* (the inhabited earth) and *shĕʾôl* (the subterranean spirit world, etc.) and to the English term "hell," all three of which regularly occur without the definite article; also the English word "heaven" (in the singular) is ordinarily used without the article. The lack of the article may be due to the fact that *tĕhôm* is used almost exclusively in poetry, being found in prose only four times out of thirty-five passages.

Though coming from the same root, the two words do not denote the same thing. This is nothing surprising, for root relationship does not itself prove identity in meaning. We can illustrate this quite easily by a few well-known examples. French *actuellement* ("at present") and German *selig* ("blessed") are derived from the same roots as English "actually" and "silly," respectively. But what divergencies in meaning!

Tiʾâmat, as we have observed, is a mythical personality. Such significance the Old Testament *tĕhôm* never has. The complete lack of mythological associations appears with unmistakable clarity from Gen. 1:2: "And darkness was upon the *face* of *tĕhôm*," i.e., on the surface of the deep. If *tĕhôm* were here treated as a mythological entity, the expression "face" would have to be taken literally; but this would obviously lead to absurdity. For why should there be darkness only on the *face* of *tĕhôm* and not over the entire body? "On the face of the deep" is here used interchangeably with "on the face of the waters," which we meet at the end of the same verse. The one expression is as free from mythological connotation as is the other. In the Old Testament, *tĕhôm* is nothing but a designation for the deep, the sea, the ocean, or any large body of water; in Gen. 1:2 it refers to the vast expanse of water from which the waters above the firmament were separated on the second day and out of which the dry land emerged on the third day (cf. Ps. 104:6). But, while *tĕhôm* stands for the *entire* body of water, Tiʾâmat represents only one *part* of it, the other being represented by Apsû, who finds no mention at all in the biblical creation story.

It has been asserted that Hebrew *tĕhôm* is a derivative of Babylonian *Tiʾâmat* and that here we have a point in favor of the view that the creation story in Gen. 1:1—2:3 is dependent upon *Enûma elish*.[57] But to derive *těhôm* from *Tiʾâmat* is grammatically impossible, because the former has a masculine, the latter a feminine, ending. As a loan-word from *Tiʾâmat*, *těhôm* would need a feminine ending, in accordance with the laws of derivation from Babylonian in Hebrew. Moreover, it would have no *h*, unless it had been derived from a Babylonian form *Tihâmat*, which may have existed in Babylonian speech. Had *Tiʾâmat* been taken over into Hebrew, it would either have been left as it was or it would have been changed to *tiʾāmā* or *teʾāmā*, with the feminine ending *ā*, but it would not have become *těhôm*.[58] As far as the system of Semitic grammar is concerned, *těhôm* represents an older and more original formation than does *Tiʾâmat*, since the feminine is formed from the masculine, by the addition of the feminine ending, which in Babylonian and Assyrian appears, in its full form, as -*at*.

The only way in which we can account for the above-mentioned morphological differences between *Tiʾâmat* and *těhôm* is by assuming that both words go back to a common Semitic form. As common Semitic words, they could without any difficulty whatever have different terminations of gender, as we can see, for example, from such common Semitic words as Hebrew *ʾereṣ* ("earth") and Babylonian *ʾerṣetu*, Hebrew *nefesh* ("breath," "life," "soul") and Babylonian *napishtu*. That the two terms under consideration actually are common Semitic words, ultimately going back to one and the same form, is

---

[57] See, e.g., R. W. Rogers, *The Religion of Babylonia and Assyria* (New York, 1908), p. 137; and Morgenstern in the *American Journal of Semitic Languages and Literatures*, XXXVI, 197.

[58] The Hebrew name ᶜ*Êlām* cannot be advanced as counterargument, because the Hebrew form does not revert to Babylonian *Elamtu* but to Sumerian *Elam*, as shown by A. Poebel in the *American Journal of Semitic Languages and Literatures*, XLVIII (1931), 20–26. Nor can one invoke Babylonian * êkallu* ("palace," "temple") and Hebrew הֵיכָל to explain the *h* in *těhôm*, for both words are derived from Sumerian *é-gal*, which may have been pronounced *he-gal*, as pointed out by Poebel in *Zeitschrift für Assyriologie*, XXXIX (1929), 143–45. Furthermore, in Hebrew הֵיכָל the consonant *h* stands at the beginning, while in *těhôm* it is found in the middle, which makes a decided difference, as we can see, e.g., from the treatment of the *spiritus asper* or rough breathing in Greek compound verbs. A secondary *h* can develop at the beginning of a word (cf. Ethiopic *Hēnōs* and Hebrew ʾ*Enôsh* [Gen. 5:6–11], Ethiopic *Hagrippās* and Latin *Agrippa*); but there does not seem to be any proof that such an *h* can appear in the middle.

borne out by the fact that the same root appears again in Babylonian *tâmtu* (which occasionally interchanges with *Tiʾâmat*), in Arabic *Tihâmatu* or *Tihâma*, a name for the coastal land in western Arabia,[59] and on the tablets from Ras Shamra (on the northern coast of Syria), where we find the form *t-h-m*, meaning "the ocean" or "the deep." The occurrence of *tĕhôm* in the first chapter of Genesis is worth noting, inasmuch as it is a comparatively rare word in the Old Testament and is used chiefly in poetry, but it does not deserve much more consideration than does the occurrence of such common Semitic words as *shamâmu* ("heaven") and *ʾerṣetu* ("earth") in *Enûma elish* and *shāmayim* and *ʾereṣ* in Genesis.[60]

PRIMEVAL DARKNESS

Another correspondence between the two narratives is the idea of a primeval darkness, which is found also in the cosmologies of other ancient nations (e.g., the Phoenicians and the Greeks). In *Enûma elish* this conception is not expressly stated, but we can deduce it from the fact that Tiʾâmat, according to Berossus (pp. 77–78), was shrouded in darkness, as we saw in the preceding chapter. Moreover, Berossus says very explicitly: "There was a time in which all was darkness." But while from *Enûma elish* this idea can be inferred only with the aid of Berossus, in Genesis it is expressed in clear and unequivocal terms: "And darkness was upon the face of the deep."

LIGHT BEFORE THE LUMINARIES

Both accounts refer to the existence of light and to the alternation of day and night before the creation of the heavenly bodies. In *Enûma elish* day and night are spoken of as being already in existence at the time of Apsû's revolt against the ways of the gods, his children (Tablet I:38). Furthermore, Tablet I:68 makes mention of the radiance or dazzling aureole which surrounded Apsû. Finally, Marduk, the conqueror of Tiʾâmat and the fabricator of the world, was a solar deity, from whom

[59] Cf. R. P. Dougherty, *The Sealand of Ancient Arabia* (New Haven, 1932), p. 173.

[60] In reply to criticism, I want to emphasize that I deny the Babylonian derivation of *tĕhôm* from *Tiʾâmat* for purely grammatical reasons.

light proceeded as from a luminary; he is explicitly called the "son of the sun-god, the sun-god of the go[ds]" (Tablet I:102). In Genesis day and night are likewise mentioned as existing before the celestial bodies, but here light is a *creation* of God and not a divine *attribute*. "God said: 'Let there be light!' And there was light; and God saw that the light was good. And God separated the light from the darkness. And God called the light 'day' and the darkness He called 'night.' "

THE MARDUK-TIᵃMAT CONFLICT

In *Enûma elish* the first four tablets deal almost exclusively with the contest between Marduk and Tiᵃmat and the events leading up to it, while the creation story proper occupies less than two tablets. The Hebrew account, on the contrary, deals almost exclusively with the creation, and not a trace is found anywhere in the first two chapters of Genesis of a conflict between God and some mythical figure. No one will deny that.

Some of the poetical books of the Old Testament, however, do contain passages in which the idea of a conflict between God and some hostile elements is brought out very distinctly. In many quarters these portions of Sacred Writ are regarded as the last shattered remnants of a creation story in which God, like Marduk, was pictured as having contended with a huge monster and its helpers *before* the making of heaven and earth. The first to collect and discuss all the pertinent material was Hermann Gunkel, in his book *Schöpfung und Chaos in Urzeit und Endzeit*, published in Göttingen in 1895. The most outstanding examples advanced by Gunkel are the following ones:

ISA. 51:9–10

Awake, awake, put on strength,
  O arm of the Lord!
Awake as in the days of old,
  (as) in the generations of ancient times!
Was it not Thou that didst hew Rahab in pieces,
  that didst pierce the crocodile (*tannin*)?
Was it not Thou that didst dry up the sea,
  the waters of the great deep;
That didst make the depths of the sea a way
  for the redeemed to pass over?

Ps. 89:9–12

O Lord, God of hosts, who is strong like Thee, O Lord?
And Thy faithfulness is round about Thee.[61]
Thou rulest over the raging of the sea;
When its waves rise Thou stillest them.[62]
Thou didst crush Rahab like one who is slain;[63]
With Thy strong arm Thou didst scatter Thine enemies.
The heavens are Thine, the earth also is Thine;
The world and its fulness—Thou didst found them.

Job 9:13–14

God does not turn back His anger.
Under Him bowed the helpers of Rahab;
How much less shall *I* answer Him,
(Or) choose my words (to reason) with Him?

Job 26:12–13

By His power the sea is quiet,[64]
And by His understanding He smites[64] Rahab;
By His breath the sky is cleared,
His hand pierces[64] the fleeing serpent.

Isa. 27:1

On that day the Lord will punish
With His sword, which is hard and great and strong,
Leviathan, the fleeing serpent,[65]
And Leviathan, the tortuous serpent,
And He will slay the crocodile (*tannîn*) that is in the sea.[66]

[61] Is in evidence on every side.

[62] Cf. Ps. 65:8 and Matt. 8:23 ff.

[63] With the same ease.

[64] For this use of the perfect see *Gesenius' Hebrew Grammar*, sec. 106, *k*. The context requires the present tense in English. For the translation of רָגַע in the sense "to be quiet," "to be at rest," "to repose," see Francis Brown, S. R. Driver, and Charles A. Briggs, *A Hebrew and English Lexicon of the Old Testament* (Boston and New York, 1907), p. 921; cf. also the Septuagint translation κατέπαυσεν, "he quieted."

[65] A serpent in flight looks crooked or tortuous. If we consider this expression from that viewpoint, "the fleeing serpent" forms a beautiful parallel to "the tortuous serpent" of the next line.

[66] In this line "the sea" probably refers to the Nile, as in Isa. 19:5; Nah. 3:8, and Job 41:23 (cf. also Jer. 51:36, where "the sea" stands for the Euphrates). In Arabic the word *baḥr* denotes not only the sea but also any large river, such as the Nile, the Euphrates, and the Tigris (E. W. Lane, *An Arabic-English Lexicon*, Book I, Part 1 [London and Edinburgh, 1863], p. 156, *c*).

Ps. 74:12–17

God is my king from of old,
Who works salvation in the midst of the earth.
Thou didst divide the sea by Thy power;
Thou didst crush the heads of the crocodiles (tannînîm) by the waters.
Thou didst shatter the heads of Leviathan,
Thou didst give him as food to the desert-folk.[67]
Thou didst cleave fountain and brook,
Thou didst dry up unfailing rivers;
Day and night are both Thine,
Thou didst establish the light and the sun.
Summer and winter—Thou didst make them.

Here, then, we have unmistakable references to a conflict between God and some hostile beings—Rahab, Leviathan, the serpent, and the crocodile. But what is meant by these terms, particularly by "Rahab" and "Leviathan"? The sense of these expressions cannot be established with mathematical precision, but we have some very good indications as to their general meaning.

Let us begin with "Rahab." In Isa. 51:9 this word forms a parallel to tannîn, which denotes a long-bodied creature and is used in the Old Testament for the serpent, the crocodile, and evidently also for such sea monsters as the whale and the shark (cf. Gen. 1:21; Ps. 148:7); in Isa. 51:9 tannîn is no doubt to be taken in the sense of "crocodile," because of the relation which that passage bears to Egypt, as we shall see. "Rahab" is found again in Job 26:12 f. This passage consists of two couplets, which, in turn, form a quatrain, in which the first line corresponds to the third and the second line to the fourth. Accordingly, "Rahab" in this text forms a parallel not only to the sea but also to the fleeing serpent. From the fact that in verse 12 "Rahab" parallels the sea, Gunkel[68] concluded that Rahab was identical with the sea. But this deduction does not agree with the context. How these two lines must be interpreted is shown by verse 13. There the fleeing serpent is not the sky itself, rather

[67] I.e., the beasts of the desert (cf. Prov. 30:25 f., where עַם, "people," "folk," is applied to the ants and the rock badgers).

[68] Schöpfung und Chaos in Urzeit und Endzeit (Göttingen, 1895), pp. 36 f. (cf. also ibid., pp. 91 ff.).

it is a *feature of* the sky, something *in* the sky. It may be either the dragon which the ancients associated with eclipses,[69] or perhaps a poetical personification of the clouds that move across the sky.[70] The latter interpretation seems preferable in view of the statement: "By His breath [i.e., His wind] the sky is cleared." In like manner "Rahab" cannot be identified with the sea but must be regarded as something *in* the sea; it must refer to a huge marine creature. The sense of verse 12, then, is that God is master over the sea and the most formidable creature found in it. In Isa. 30:7 and Ps. 87:4 "Rahab" occurs as a designation of Egypt, which resembled a gigantic serpent, or a crocodile, stretching far along the sea. The same term is evidently also applied to Egypt in Ps. 89:11 and in Job 9:13. Both verses doubtless refer to Israel's passage through the Red Sea, when God not only revealed his power over the waters of the sea, so that by the blast of his nostrils "the streams stood up like a heap (and) the floods were congealed in the heart of the sea" (Exod. 15:8), but also scattered and destroyed the Egyptians and rescued his people from the power of their enemies (Exod. 14:23–31; 15:6), while "the helpers of Rahab," i.e., either the gods of Egypt (cf. Exod. 12:12; also 15:11) or her mighty warriors,[71] unable to avert the disaster, had to admit defeat and, as it were, bow under the God of the Hebrews.[72] From these references it is clear that "Rahab" is a synonymous term for the serpent and the crocodile.

The term "Leviathan" occurs in Job, chapter 41 (Job 40:25—41:26 in the Hebrew text), not in reference to some mythical monster of the past but, as attested by the context, of an actual living animal of the present; it is used as a designation of the crocodile, which is there described in poetic language,

---

[69] With regard to the superstition which this explanation seems to involve, it should be remembered, first, that we may have before us a mere metaphor and, second, that Job was not a member of the tribes of Israel.

[70] Cf. König, *Das Buch Hiob* (Gütersloh, 1929), p. 257.

[71] With the latter possibility cf. Ps. 89:11, where "Rahab" is paralleled by "Thine enemies," i.e., the Egyptians or the armed forces of Egypt.

[72] The argument that such a direct reference to an event in the history of Egypt and Israel would be contrary to the character of the Book of Job is quite inconclusive. There are exceptions to every rule.

even as breathing fire and smoke.[73] This application of the word
is in full accord with the etymology of the name. "Leviathan"
is an adjectival formation, and means, as far as can be determined, something coiled or wreathed (cf. *liwyā*, "wreath," Prov.
1:9; 4:9). The term apparently alludes to the rows of scales that
cover the body of the crocodile.[74] In Job 3:8 "Leviathan" probably refers either to the dragon which in ancient times was believed to produce eclipses by swallowing the sun or the moon or
by surrounding it in its coils,[75] or to the clouds that hide the sun
and the moon.[76] In Isa. 27:1 "Leviathan" is called "the fleeing
serpent" and "the tortuous serpent." These two epithets are
synonymous with "the *tannîn* (the crocodile) that is in the sea,"
as in Ps. 74:14, where Leviathan forms a parallel to "the *tannînîm* (the crocodiles) by the waters."[77] From Ps. 104:25 f. we
learn that Leviathan was created to frolic in "the sea great and
broad." If by this expression is meant the Mediterranean, then
"Leviathan" can hardly stand for the crocodile, since the crocodile is a sweet-water animal; the allusion is then in all probability to some cetacean animal. However, it is far more likely that
"the sea great and broad" was intended as a designation for the
Nile, which in Isa, 19:5 and Nah. 3:8 very clearly bears the
appellation the "sea" and which even to the present day is
called by the Arabs *el-Baḥr*, "the Sea."

[73] This poetic description, however, agrees remarkably well with prosaic reality
(see Eduard Hertlein in *Zeitschrift für die alttestamentliche Wissenschaft*, XXXVIII
[1919/20], 148 f.; S. R. Driver and G. B. Gray, *A Critical and Exegetical Commentary on the Book of Job* [New York, 1921], I, 359–71; König, *Das Buch Hiob*, pp.
432–46).

[74] The underlying root of the name in question appears also in the Babylonian-
Assyrian words *lawû* or *lamû*, "to surround," "to enclose"; *limêtu*, "environs"; and
lamûtânu, "slave," "servant."

[75] See Driver and Gray, *op. cit.*, pp. 33 f., and E. B. Tylor, *Primitive Culture*
(New York, 1924), I, 328–35.

[76] König, *Das Buch Hiob*, pp. 61 f.

[77] The term *tannîn* occurs also in the literature of Ras Shamra, where in one
passage it parallels, or is equated with, Shalyaṭ, an epithet of Lôtan, i.e., Leviathan. Albright, in the *Bulletin of the American Schools of Oriental Research*, No. 84
(1941), 16, has rendered the passage in question as follows:

I muzzled Tannin, I muzzled him(?)!
I have destroyed the winding serpent,
Shalyaṭ of the seven heads.

We have seen that both Rahab and Leviathan are paralleled with the crocodile; in fact, that Leviathan is actually identified with the crocodile. We have also seen that Rahab is, moreover, paralleled with the "fleeing serpent" and that the "fleeing serpent" is Leviathan. This interchange of terms shows quite definitely that "Rahab" and "Leviathan" are synonyms.

From these observations it is apparent that "Rahab" and "Leviathan" are properly terms for real animals but that they are also employed for imaginary entities closely resembling the animals with which these names originated. Thus in Job 26:12 "Rahab" denotes a real aquatic creature of some kind, and in Job, chapter 41, "Leviathan" is obviously used of an actual crocodile. Also in Ps. 104:25–29 a real animal is meant by "Leviathan." For there it is stated, as we have seen in part, that Leviathan was formed by the Lord to play in the sea and that together with the innumerable creatures that swarm therein this great monster waits upon the Lord for its food. But in Ps. 74:14, where the poet speaks of "the *heads* of Leviathan," the picture is that of an imaginary monster, a sort of Greek Hydra.

The latter interpretation of "Leviathan" finds strong confirmation on a tablet excavated some years ago at Ras Shamra.[78] In a battle scene recorded on the first column of that inscription a certain deity is addressing another one, saying:

"When thou shalt smite Lôtan, the fleeing serpent,
(And) shalt put an end to the tortuous serpent,
Shalyaṭ of the seven heads. . . . . ."[79]

In this myth Lôtan has seven heads; this shows that he is here pictured as a fabulous ophidian being. The seven-headed serpent is mentioned in Old Babylonian lists and omens and in the bilingual epic *Andimdimma*, in which the weapon of the god Ninurta is compared with this monster.[80] Furthermore, such a

[78] See Ch. Virolleaud in *Syria, revue d'art oriental et d'archéologie*, XV (1934), 305–36; J. A. Montgomery and Z. S. Harris, *The Ras Shamra Mythological Texts* (Philadelphia, 1935), pp. 39 ff. and 78 ff.

[79] With the translation cf. Cyrus H. Gordon, *Ugaritic Handbook* (Rome, 1947), pp. 91 f., and Albright in the *Bulletin of the American Schools of Oriental Research*, No. 83 (1941), 39 f.

[80] See Landsberger, *Die Fauna des alten Mesopotamien* (Leipzig, 1934), p. 60, *o*.

serpent is represented on a Sumerian macehead (Fig. 15);[81] and on a seal coming from Tell Asmar (ancient Eshnunna), fifty miles northeast of modern Baghdad, and dating back to about the middle of the third millennium B.C., is a dragon with seven serpent heads (Fig. 16).[82]

The passage from Ras Shamra at the same time shows that "Leviathan" denotes a creation of fancy also in Isa. 27:1:

> On that day the Lord will punish
> With His sword, which is hard and great and strong,
> Leviathan, the fleeing serpent,[83]
> And Leviathan, the tortuous serpent,[83]
> And He will slay the crocodile that is in the sea.

On the basis of these considerations, however, we cannot conclude that God is anywhere represented as actually at war with *monsters*, as is Marduk in *Enûma elish;* for in all the Old Testament passages which speak of a struggle between the Almighty, on the one hand, and Rahab, Leviathan, and their variant designations, on the other, the terms under consideration are mere figures of speech applied to powerful nations which are hostile to God or his people, although we may not always be able at this remote point of time to determine with certainty what particular nation is meant.[84] We can see this quite clearly from Ps. 87:4 and Isa. 30:7, where "Rahab" occurs as a poetical name for Egypt;[85] from Ezek. 29:3 and 32:2, where the king of Egypt

---

[81] Frankfort in *Analecta orientalia*, No. 12 (1935), p. 108.

[82] Frankfort, *Iraq Excavations of the Oriental Institute, 1932/33* (Chicago, 1934), p. 49. Howard Wallace, in the *Biblical Archaeologist*, XI (1948), 63, seems to be of the opinion that Leviathan is everywhere a seven-headed serpent, for he writes: "We know that Leviathan is a seven headed serpent connected with water." In Job 40:25—41:26 (according to the Hebrew text), Leviathan has very definitely only one head, since the poet speaks of his tongue, nose, jaw, *head*, and mouth in the *singular*.

[83] The Hebrew text has נָחָשׁ for "serpent," while the passage from Ras Shamra has a word which etymologically corresponds to the less frequent Hebrew term פֶּתֶן.

[84] See König, *Bibel und Babel* (Berlin, 1902), pp. 25 ff., and *"Altorientalische Weltanschauung" und Altes Testament* (Gr. Lichterfelde-Berlin [1905]), pp. 39–43; Aloys Kirchner, *Die babylonische Kosmogonie und der biblische Schöpfungsbericht* (Münster i.W., 1911), pp. 27–45; Morris Jastrow, Jr., *Hebrew and Babylonian Traditions* (New York, 1914), p. 115; Hertlein in *Zeitschrift für die alttestamentliche Wissenschaft*, XXXVIII, 113–54; and Aug. Bea in *Biblica*, XIX (1938), 444 ff.

[85] On Isa. 30:7 see König, *Das Buch Jesaja* (Gütersloh, 1926), pp. 271 f.

is expressly called "the great *tannîn* (or *tannîm*)" and a "*tannîm* in the seas," respectively; and from Isa. 51:9 f. and Ps. 74:12–16. The last two passages unquestionably refer to the occasion of Israel's passing through the Red Sea. As far as Isa. 51:9 f. is concerned, this point emerges with great clarity from the fact that in verse 9 the poet calls on God to display his power not as in the period before the creation but "(as) in the *generations of ancient times*" (i.e., in *historic* times, long *after* the advent of man) and from verse 10: "Was it not Thou that didst dry up the sea, the waters of the great deep; that didst make the depths of the sea a way for the redeemed to pass over?" The event here alluded to did not coincide with the creation of the world, for at that time the sea was *not* dried up, neither according to *Enûma elish* nor according to Genesis; but it *was* dried up in the days of the Exodus. Hence the "redeemed" are the same of whom the poet, in his hymn of victory, sings: "In Thy mercy Thou hast led the people whom Thou hast redeemed" (Exod. 15:13).[86] That the same experience, together with some of the subsequent events, is referred to also in Ps. 74:12–16 is obvious in the light of Exod. 14:15–30; 15:6 f.; 17:6; Num. 20:8; and Josh. 3:17.[87] In Isa. 51:9 f. and Ps. 74:12–16 Rahab, Leviathan, and the crocodiles are clearly emblematic designations for Egypt and the Egyptians. Also in Isa. 27:1 the allusion evidently is to earthly kingdoms or powers, the expressions "the fleeing serpent," "the tortuous serpent," and "the crocodile" probably being metaphors for Assyria (situated along the swift-running Tigris), Babylonia (along the winding Euphrates), and Egypt (symbolized by the crocodile in the sea, i.e., in the Nile), respectively.[88]

[86] Since in the same hymn (vss. 5–10) the waters of the Red Sea are called "mighty waters" and *têhômôth*, there is no reason why they could not equally well be designated as *mê thêhôm rabbâ*, "the waters of the great deep," inasmuch as the latter phrase has the same force as the plural *têhômôth* (*Gesenius' Hebrew Grammar*, sec. 124). This form—*têhômôth*—we encounter again in Ps. 106:9 and Isa 63:13, which likewise treat of Israel's passage through the Red Sea.

[87] See also Franz Delitzsch, *Biblical Commentary on the Psalms*, trans. D. Eaton, II (New York, n.d.), 382 f.; C. A. Briggs, *A Critical and Exegetical Commentary on the Book of Psalms*, I (New York, 1907), 155; and König, *Die Psalmen* (Gütersloh, 1927), pp. 670 f.

[88] See A. Dillmann, *Der Prophet Jesaja*, rev. and ed. by R. Kittel (Leipzig, 1898), pp. 239 f., and König, *Das Buch Jesaja*, pp. 242 f.

Friedrich Delitzsch[89] held that Isa. 51:9 f. has reference to
the supposed conflict between God and a mythical figure called
"Rahab" and that the prophet coupled these mythical reflections with Israel's deliverance from the bondage of Egypt, as
another triumph of God over the waters of the deep, or the
těhôm. But, as we shall see more clearly in the course of this discussion, there is no justification whatever for this assumption;
it certainly cannot be found in the fact that the destruction of
Rahab and the piercing of the crocodile is placed in "the days
of old" (yěmê qedem), for this very same phrase is used in Mic.
7:20 to designate the age of the patriarchs, while in Isa. 63:11
the days of Moses are even referred to as "the days of eternity"
(yěmê ʿôlām). The simplest and most natural interpretation of
Isa. 51:9 f. is to regard "Rahab" and the crocodile as metaphor-
ical terms for Egypt. Parallels to this use of metaphors in poetic
writings are found in Isa. 30:6 and in Amos 4:1; in the former
passage the Egyptians are referred to as "the beasts of the
south," and in the latter the prophet addresses the women of
Samaria by the uncomplimentary phrase "Ye cows of Bashan."
Further examples are the "bulls" and "dogs" in Psalm 22 and
the "wolves" and "lions" in Zeph. 3:3 (cf. also Isa. 14:29 and
Dan. 7:3 ff.).

But whence did the prophets and poets derive this imagery?
The assertion has been made by Gunkel[90] and others that Rahab, Leviathan, etc., are synonymous with the "dragon"
Tiʾâmat and the monsters associated with her and that the biblical passages under discussion are echoes of Marduk's victory
over Tiʾâmat and her forces. In support of this contention reference has been made to the fact that God shattered the heads of
Leviathan (Ps. 74:14) and hewed Rahab in pieces and pierced
the crocodile (Isa. 51:9), that with his skill or understanding he
smote Rahab and slew the fleeing serpent (Job 26:12 f.), that
with his strong arm he scattered his enemies (Ps. 89:11), that
under him the helpers of Rahab bowed (Job 9:13), and that he
threatens to spread his net over the crocodile (the king of
Egypt) and to draw it up in his seine (Ezek. 32:3); these

[89] Babel and Bible, p. 160.

[90] Schöpfung und Chaos . . . . , pp. 29 ff.

phrases are said to be reflections of the Babylonian story relating how Marduk, the wise and skilful, caught Tiᵖâmat in his net, how he pierced her with the arrow of his bow, how he smashed her skull and cut her body in two, how he broke her band and dispersed her host, and how he finally vanquished her helpers and trampled them underfoot (Tablet IV:93 ff.).

While we cannot raise any valid objections against the general idea that the sacred writers of the Old Testament could or might have derived, whether directly or indirectly, certain figures of speech from the Babylonian myth of the Marduk-Tiᵖâmat fight in order to illustrate truth, provided that this story was sufficiently well known is Israel (for otherwise the allusions to it would have had little force and significance), an examination of the correspondences between the biblical passages in question and the Babylonian story will readily reveal that the similarities are by no means strong enough to show that they actually did so in this case, especially since the supposed allusions are found in *different* books of the Bible. The only points which might impress one at first sight are the use of the net, the mention of the helpers of Rahab, the fact that Tiᵖâmat in *Enûma elish* and Rahab in the Old Testament are punished more severely than their helpers, and the general idea of a conflict between good and evil. A moment's reflection, however, will show that even these similarities carry no weight. The net was known to both nations; the phrase "the helpers of Rahab," which is reminiscent of the helpers of Tiᵖâmat, may have arisen independently, especially if we consider that *Rahab* had become a poetical name for Egypt and that "the helpers of Rahab" may refer either to the gods of Egypt or to her warriors, as we have pointed out; the fact that the ring leaders are punished more severely than are their helpers is just what we should expect in any story of this type, and the further fact that both *Enûma elish* and the Old Testament contain the idea of a conflict between good and evil does not prove anything either as far as the sources of the biblical passages are concerned, because that idea is universal. Furthermore, it still remains to be proved, as we have observed, that Tiᵖâmat was a dragon or a dragon-like creature. It is, of course, *possible* that Tiᵖâmat, in spite of the fact that she was a woman and the mother of the gods, was in later times portrayed as a dragon, just as Satan, the chief of the fallen angels, is designated in Rev. 12:9 as "the great dragon" and "that old serpent." But we have no proof that such a thing was actually done in the case of Ti᾽âmat, whether in Babylonia or in Palestine.

Some of these figures of speech the Hebrews obviously derived from traditions current in the West, as evidenced by the unusually close correspondences between Isa. 27:1, Ps. 74:14, and the text from Ras Shamra. But whether they derived them from North Syrian documents directly or whether they received them through the channels of a long oral tradition, we cannot tell. Nor does it matter, as we shall see. Furthermore, we have no assurance as to whether these traditions originated somewhere in the West or whether they must ultimately be traced back to Babylonia. Neither does this matter. The idea of the seven-headed serpent would seem to have emanated from Babylonia. But while some of these Old Testament figures of speech are no doubt due to foreign influence of some kind, others may quite as well have been suggested to the sacred writers by their own observation of nature. The statement made by Jensen almost half a century ago still stands, viz.: "When the Old Testament speaks of a conflict of Yahweh [or Jehovah] against creatures resembling serpents and crocodiles, there is no occasion to assume, with Delitzsch and an imposing number of other Assyriologists, a connection with the Babylonian myth of the Ti᾽âmat conflict."[91]

It now remains to inquire *when* God engaged in these conflicts. As we saw above, in many circles it is held that they took place *before* the creation of the world, on the grounds that in some passages acts of creation are mentioned immediately *after* God's victorious combat.[92] Attention has been drawn to such passages as Ps. 89:9–12 and 74:12–17, where the founding of "the world and its fulness," the establishment of light and sun, and the fixing of "all the bounds of the earth" are spoken of *after* the slaying of Rahab and Leviathan. But that alone proves

[91] Translated from *Die christliche Welt*, Vol. XVI (1902), col. 490.

[92] See Gunkel, *Schöpfung und Chaos* . . . . , pp. 29 ff.; Clay, *Light on the Old Testament from Babel* (Philadelphia, 1907), pp. 69–71; Rogers, *op. cit.*, pp. 133–36.

nothing. What evidence do we possess that the order in which these acts are described was intended to be chronological? If the mere order in which these things are recorded is a decisive criterion for chronological sequence, then it follows that in both instances Gunkel's hypothesis is definitely not in agreement with the context. For in Psalm 89 the poet plainly speaks *first* of the present (vs. 10), and *then* he mentions the crushing of Rahab (vs. 11). And in Psalm 74 the poet extols God's works of salvation "in the midst of the *earth*," i.e., the salvation which he wrought *after* the earth had been brought into existence. This is confirmed by verse 14*b* ("Thou didst give him as food to the desert-folk"), which shows very distinctly that the recorded conflict dates from the time *after* the creation of the desert and its inhabitants and hence *after* the creation of the earth. Moreover, in the same psalm the dividing of the sea, which work is itself an act of creation according to *Enûma elish* and Genesis, is mentioned *before* the destruction of Leviathan.[93] In both psalms the context shows quite clearly that the poet is not at all concerned about chronology; he simply picks out at random some of the mighty deeds of God to exemplify his omnipotent power without regard for chronological sequence. If Psalm 89, for example, were really meant to be a chronological enumeration of events, verse 11*b* would even have to come before verse 11*a*. Furthermore, in Isa. 51:9 f., which admittedly refers to Israel's deliverance from Egypt and her passage through the Red Sea, when God hewed Rahab in pieces and pierced the crocodile, this conflict very obviously takes place *after* creation. And in Isa. 27:1 the encounter is still in the future. Finally, in the aforementioned inscription from Ras Shamra the fight with Lôtan is likewise joined *after* creation, as we can discern from column i, lines 14–17, where one of the gods says:

> "(It is) his will[94] that a sheep excite the desire of a lioness,
> Or the appetite of a dolphin in the sea.
> (And yet) behold, my knees overtook wild bulls,
> . . . they have overtaken hinds!"[95]

[93] In the Babylonian conflict, of which these passages are said to be a reflection, Ti'âmat is killed first and then divided.

[94] The will of the death-god.

[95] The rendition is that of Albright in the *Bulletin of the American Schools of Oriental Research*, No. 83, pp. 41 f.

This statement is made while Lôtan is still at large, and while the combat is still in the future, as shown by lines 26–31. This proves, of course, that the tablet from Ras Shamra *presupposes* the creation of the world. In this respect the above myth from Ras Shamra corresponds to the Babylonian tradition of Enlil and a monster named *labbu* and to the myth of the Zû-bird (see Appendix); in both cases the fight *follows* the creation. There is, accordingly, no evidence in these Bible passages of a conflict *preceding* the creation, but there are very good reasons for placing these struggles *after* the creation. The whole theory of a Hebrew cosmogony in which the making of heaven and earth was preceded by a contest between the Creator and certain monsters, as in *Enûma elish*, thus falls to the ground.[96]

After this digression let us now return to the Book of Genesis and continue our points of comparison between the various Babylonian versions of creation and the first two chapters of the Old Testament.

THE CREATION OF THE FIRMAMENT

The next point of contact between *Enûma elish* and Genesis, chapter 1, is found in connection with the creation of the firmament. Both accounts agree that this act was accompanied by a division of primeval waters. *Enûma elish* speaks of three different types of waters: there was Apsû, the sweet-water ocean; Tiʾâmat, the salt-water ocean; and Mummu, apparently representing the fog, the mist, and the clouds, which rose from Apsû and Tiʾâmat and hovered over them. The waters of Apsû and Mummu were disposed of by Ea before the birth of Marduk. For we have seen that Ea slew Apsû and established his abode

---

[96] R. H. Pfeiffer's contention, in the *Journal of Bible and Religion*, X (1942), 246 f., that G. Sarton, in *Osiris*, II (1936), 406–60, has shown "the fight with the dragon" to be "the most characteristic element common to the ancient Mediterranean world," is so decidedly at variance with the facts that his appeal to this article is difficult to understand. In the first place, Sarton's study is "devoted to the highest cultural achievements of the Middle Ages, especially to those which occurred in the period extending from the eighth century to the thirteenth" (p. 406). And, in the second place, Sarton barely touches on the dragon fight, dedicating about a dozen lines to it on p. 459 and probably alluding to it in a few more lines on the next page—out of a total of about fifty-five pages.

on the waters of the latter, while he seized Mummu for himself and held him by his nose-rope, which plainly indicates that now the waters of Mummu were in some way brought under the control of Ea, the god of the deep (Tablet I: 59–72). The only waters which were still beyond the control of the younger gods were those of Tiᵖâmat. These waters were conquered by Marduk and were then divided by him. From one half of Tiᵖâmat he formed the earth and from the other half he formed the sky, or the firmament. Moreover, he fixed the crossbar and posted guards, commanding them not to let the celestial waters escape (Tablet IV: 128–45).

In Genesis, God creates a firmament "in the middle of the waters" to cause a division between the waters under the firmament and the waters above it (cf. also Ps. 148:4). The biblical account appears to imply that the waters of the earth and those of the clouds originally commingled, like the waters of Apsû, Mummu, and Tiᵖâmat, without a clear intervening air space, thus producing a condition like that obtaining during a dense fog on the water. Of what the firmament was made is not stated in Genesis.

Noteworthy as this parallel may seem, it alone does not establish the source of the biblical account. For, in the first place, the general view that the creation of heaven and earth was accomplished in part by a process of division or separation is "common property of almost all cosmogonies."[97] Thus in Egypt the air-god Shû separated heaven and earth by lifting the sky-goddess Nût from the earth-god Geb and placing himself between the two,[98] while according to Phoenician and Indian speculation the cosmic egg or world egg split into heaven and earth.[99] And, in the second place, the concept of a primeval watery chaos is met with also elsewhere, as we have observed above.

[97] W. Wundt, *Elemente der Völkerpsychologie* (Leipzig, 1913), p. 387 (cf. *ibid.*, p. 383).

[98] Cf. H. and H. A. Frankfort in H. and H. A. Frankfort, John A. Wilson, T. Jacobsen, and W. A. Irwin, *The Intellectual Adventure of Ancient Man* (Chicago, 1947), pp. 17–19.

[99] See Skinner, *op. cit.*, pp. 48–50, and F. Lukas, *Die Grundbegriffe in den Kosmogonien der alten Völker* (Leipzig, 1893), pp. 88 ff.

THE CREATION OF THE EARTH

The creation of the earth as related in the first chapter of Genesis finds its counterpart in *Enûma elish*, Tablets IV:143–45 and VII:135, and in the excerpt from Berossus. After Marduk had fashioned the sky and thus had got rid of one half of the gigantic body of Tiʾâmat, the way was clear for the formation of the earth. Thereupon Marduk measured the dimensions of the *Apsû*, i.e., the subterranean sea, and with the other half of Tiʾâmat's body made a great structure in the shape of a canopy, or a vault, and placed this hemisphere over the sea, upon which the Babylonians imagined the earth to rest. The material out of which the earth was made had existed from eternity; but Marduk evidently separated this material from the primeval salt-water ocean, personified by Tiʾâmat, and created the dry land.[100] In the first chapter of Genesis the earth was created "in the beginning," but, as in *Enûma elish*, it was covered with water, from which it was not separated until the third day, when the waters were "gathered together unto one place" and the dry land appeared.

THE CREATION OF THE LUMINARIES

From the opening lines of Tablet V we can derive another parallel. After Marduk had formed the sky and the earth, he turned his attention to the creation of the celestial bodies and to the regulation of time. He set up the signs of the zodiac, determined the year, and defined the divisions; for each of the twelve months he set up three constellations and determined the days of the year by means of the constellations. The moon he caused to shine forth and intrusted the night to her, thus making her, in a sense, the "ruler" over the night; he appointed this beautiful ornament of the night to determine or make known the days of the month. The existence of the sun is assumed in the description of the moon's relations to the sun and in the reference to the "gates on both sides" (i.e., east and west), through which the sun was believed to pass each day. The first chapter of Genesis, on the other hand, states that God created the sun,

---

[100] For a number of divergent Sumerian speculations on the origin of heaven and earth see Jacobsen in the *Journal of Near Eastern Studies*, V, 138–41.

the moon, and the stars in the firmament of the sky to separate day from night, to serve as signs, as seasons, as days and years, and to shed light on the earth; the sun was to rule the day, the moon the night. In both accounts the main purposes of the luminaries are plainly stated; they were to yield light and to serve as time dividers and time regulators. These are functions with which every nation is acquainted. In both accounts, moreover, the production of the heavenly bodies is described from the geocentric standpoint, as in all antiquity. But while Genesis follows the well-known order sun, moon, and stars, *Enûma elish* refers to the celestial bodies in the reverse order—stars, moon, and sun, perhaps because of the great significance of the stars in the lives of the astronomically and astrologically minded Babylonians. Again, while the Babylonian narrative speaks of the luminary bodies and their purposes in astronomical terms interwoven with mythology, the Hebrew account uses the language of the layman and is free from all mythological references. Finally, the idea of gates on the eastern and western horizon through which the sun entered and departed is, of course, foreign to Genesis, chapters 1 and 2.

THE CREATION OF PLANT AND ANIMAL LIFE

To date, no portion of *Enûma elish* has been recovered which contains an account of the creation of vegetation, of animals, birds, reptiles, and fishes.[101] The opinion is frequently voiced that this act may have been recorded on the missing portion of Tablet V, of which only about 22 lines out of probably 140 have been preserved. But the missing lines of Tablet V must have contained some more astronomical material as well as a section dealing with the plea of the gods to which Tablet VI:1 refers; and whether in between that there was any space left for an account of the creation of plant and animal life is questionable. The creation of vegetation is, however, referred to on Tablet VII:2, where Marduk is called "the creator of grain and legumes" (but without the slightest hint as to when these things were created), and in the bilingual version of the creation of the

---

[101] Naturally leaving out of consideration the monsters which Tiˀâmat created to help her in her conflict.

world by Marduk (pp. 62–63), while the creation of animals is briefly recorded in a version which in this volume bears the title "The Creation of Living Creatures" (p. 64), in the bilingual story just cited, and on the Sumerian fragment from Nippur (pp. 71–72). Moreover, Berossus (p. 78) says that Bēl (i.e., Marduk) formed "animals capable of bearing the air." Berossus probably derived this idea from some Babylonian tradition other than *Enûma elish*.

THE CREATION OF MAN

Of the creation of man we have quite a number of Babylonian versions. On Tablet VI:1–38 of *Enûma elish* man's creation is ascribed to Marduk and Ea; Marduk conceived the plan and imparted it to his father, Ea, who put it into execution "in accordance with the ingenious plans" of his son. Kingu, the leader of Tiᵓâmat's host, was slaughtered, and with his blood, which was mixed with earth, as Berossus says, Ea fashioned mankind, with the assistance of certain other gods, as shown by lines 31–33. On Tablet VII:29–32, however, it is stated that Marduk created mankind, whereas in reality he merely instructed Ea to do it. This diversity can quite easily be explained by the old Latin maxim *Qui facit per alium, facit per se* ("What our agent does we do ourselves"). The bilingual version of the creation of the world by Marduk (pp. 62–63) also attributes the work of man's creation to Marduk, but here Marduk is assisted by the goddess Aruru. One version makes Ea the sole creator of man (pp. 65–66). In another tradition (p. 67) it is stated that Ninḫursag (i.e., Mami) made mankind with the flesh and blood of a slain god, which she mixed with clay.[102] In still another version (pp. 68–71) we are told that Anu, Enlil, Shamash, and Ea, together with the Anunnaki, formed mankind with the blood of

---

[102] In the Atraḫasis Epic the same goddess fashions human beings from clay after the Flood, apparently to make possible a more speedy repopulation of the earth (see the writer's book *The Gilgamesh Epic and Old Testament Parallels* [Chicago, 1949], pp. 106 ff.). Clay was used also when Aruru created Enkidu as a rival to Gilgamesh, the semidivine king of Uruk (see *ibid.*, p. 19). For a number of Sumerian parallels see Kramer, *Sumerian Mythology*, pp. 68–72, and Jacobsen in the *Journal of Near Eastern Studies*, V, 143.

"(two) Lamga gods." Since man was fashioned with divine blood, Berossus says, he is rational and partakes of divine understanding. From this statement as well as from the further consideration that ancient oriental thought conceived of blood as being the seat of life, it is apparent, moreover, that the Babylonians traced the element of life in man back to the divine blood employed at his creation. A radically different conception of the origin of man is attested by several Sumerian traditions[103] and by the bilingual story which in this book bears the title "Another Account of the Creation of Man" (reverse, l. 20); here man is pictured as sprouting from the soil as if a plant.

The first chapter of Genesis records the creation of man in the following terms: "And God said: 'Let us make man in our image, after our likeness, and let them have dominion over the fish of the sea, and over the fowl of the air, and over the cattle, and over all the earth, and over every creeping thing that creeps upon the earth.' So God created man in His own image, in the image of God created He him; male and female created He them" (vss. 26 f.). And in the second chapter we read: "And the Lord God formed the man from the dust[104] of the ground, and breathed[105] into his nostrils the breath of life, and the man became a living soul" (vs. 7). "And the Lord God caused a deep sleep to fall upon man, and he slept; and He took one of his ribs and closed up its place with flesh. And the rib which He had taken from the man the Lord God built up into a woman, and brought her to the man" (vss. 21 f.). The same God who conceived the idea of creating man carries out also the actual work connected therewith.

Both in *Enûma elish* and in Gen. 1:1—2:3 the formation of man constitutes the final act of creation, or the last entity brought into being. Moreover, both accounts contain clear indications of the high importance of this act. As it is stated after Marduk's victory over Tiᵖâmat that he examined her dead body "to create ingenious things" with it (Tablet IV:136), the con-

[103] See Jacobsen in the *Journal of Near Eastern Studies*, V, 134–37.

[104] Or "the soil."

[105] Or "blew."

templation resulting in the production of heaven and earth, so it is said that, before Marduk proceeded to the creation of man, his heart prompted him "to create ingenious things" (Tablet VI:2). In the repetition of this phrase King[106] rightly sees an indication of the great significance which the Babylonians attached to this part of the story. King's deduction is corroborated by the high admiration with which the Babylonian mythographers view the completed work; for they describe man's creation as a "work not suited to (human) understanding" (Tablet VI:37). In the introductory chapter of Genesis the importance of man's creation is evidenced by the solemnity with which it is attended and by the fact that man is made in the image of God and is given dominion over earth, air, and sea. In fact, these considerations show that here the creation of man is the culminating point of the whole story.

The purpose of man's creation is conditioned by the general purpose of the universe. According to *Enûma elish*, the universe was created for the benefit of the gods. Ea built the *Apsû* as his dwelling and appointed it for shrines (Tablet I:69–76). After Marduk had completed heaven and earth, he assigned the sky to Anu, the air and the surface of the earth to Enlil, and the sweet waters in and on the earth to Ea, to serve as their residences (cf. our note on Tablet I:146). Next, Marduk established "stations" for the great gods in the skies (Tablet V). Finally, he "ingeniously" arranged the ways of the Anunnaki by dividing them into two groups and placing three hundred of them in the heavens and an equal number in the underworld (Tablet VI:9 f. and 39–44). Even Babylon was built for the gods (Tablet VI:49–73). In full agreement with these divine aims, man's creation was conceived and executed not as an end in itself or as a natural sequel to the formation of the rest of the universe but rather as an expedient to satisfy a group of discontented gods. Man's purpose in life was to be the service of the gods. As we have seen in connection with Tablet IV:120, this service had originally been imposed on the defeated rebel gods. But, upon their request, Marduk decided to relieve the vanquished and imprisoned divinities and to create man and place

[106] *The Seven Tablets of Creation*, I, liii.

him in charge of this service. Man was made to be the servant of the gods, to be a kind of breadwinner of his divine masters, and to be the builder and caretaker of their sanctuaries. In the initial chapter of Genesis man was to be the lord of the earth, the sea, and the air. The luminaries were created for the earth, and the earth was created for man. The situation depicted in the biblical story is beautifully expressed in Ps. 115:16: "The heavens are the heavens of the Lord, but the earth has He given to the children of men." A certain degree of human dominion over creation is understood in the Babylonian account, for this is implied in Tablet VI:107–20, which charges man with the building of sanctuaries and the bringing of offerings. But, in the first place, this is not expressly stated. And, in the second place, it is the dominion or authority of a *servant*, not of a lord. Each account stresses an entirely different aspect of man's place in nature.

In "A Bilingual Version of the Creation of the World by Marduk," man is likewise made for the sake of the gods. There the gods solemnly proclaim Babylon as the dwelling of their hearts' delight; but, in order to induce them to stay there, Marduk and Aruru create the race of men so that these might attend to the needs of the gods by building their sanctuaries and maintaining their sacrifices. According to a third version, which we have entitled "Another Account of the Creation of Man" (pp. 68–71), humankind was brought into being because the gods desired to have someone to establish the boundary ditch and to keep the canals in their right courses; to irrigate the land to make it produce; to raise grain; to increase ox, sheep, cattle, fish, and fowl; to build sanctuaries for the gods; and to celebrate their festivals. All this man was to do for the benefit of his divine overlords, because "the service of the gods" was his "portion." A similarity to this last tradition is found in the second chapter of Genesis, which mentions as man's destiny the cultivation of the soil (vs. 5) and the development and preservation of the Garden of Eden (vs. 15). But this work obviously was in his own interest; the Lord God did not ask for any returns. Man's purpose in life was not idleness and useless enjoyment but pleasant and profitable work. But after the fall his work was cursed with a thousand ills. In the Babylonian stories man's creation is told from the viewpoint of the gods, while in Genesis it is told from the viewpoint of man.[107]

THE FALL OF MAN

The Book of Genesis, in conformity with the whole biblical doctrine of the nature and attributes of God, from whose hands nothing morally imperfect can possibly issue, represents man as having been created in holiness and righteousness. In the first chapter God speaks, and it is done exactly as he had commanded, everything turns out in full accord with his will. Hence man could not have been morally imperfect, for God does not will moral imperfection. Moreover, had man been created evil, God would not have signified his approval by declaring that man, like the rest of his creation, was "very good" (1:31); much less would this verdict have been introduced with a solemn "behold!" And in the second chapter it is expressly stated that the Lord God breathed into the nostrils of man "the breath of life," i.e., God's own vital breath, and so "man became a living soul" or "a living being" (2:7; cf. also Eccles. 12:7). This fact and the sequel to the story again preclude the idea of original moral imperfection in man. But man did not continue in this state of holiness; by eating of the forbidden fruit, he fell into sin.

Similar stories dealing with the fall of man are sometimes said to have been current also in Babylonia and Assyria. The most important and best known of them is the Adapa Legend, of which a translation will be found in the Appendix to this volume.

Adapa was a semidivine being, the provisioner of Ea's temple in the city of Eridu. Ea had created, or begotten, him to be a leader among men; he had granted him divine wisdom, but he had not granted him the gift of eternal life. One day, as Adapa was out on the Persian Gulf catching fish for the temple of Ea, the south wind suddenly arose, overturned his boat, and threw him into the water. Enraged at this, Adapa cursed the south wind, which the Babylonians pictured to themselves either as a bird or as some composite creature with wings, and, by uttering

---

[107] Cf. Skinner, *op. cit.*, pp. 55 and 66; Eichrodt, *op. cit.*, II, 64 f.; King, *op. cit.*, p. lxxxviii.

this curse, he broke one of the wings of the south wind, so that for seven days it did not blow the cool gulf breezes over the hot land. For this incident Adapa is called before Anu, the sky-god, to give an account of his deed. But before he ascends to heaven, Ea, his father, instructs him. He is to wear long hair and to clothe himself with a mourning garment, to excite the compassion of Tammuz and Gizzida, the gatekeepers of heaven. They will ask him the reason for his mourning, and he is to tell them that he is mourning because they, Tammuz and Gizzida, who formerly lived on earth, have disappeared from the land of the living. They will be touched by this sign of reverence for them and will intercede for him. Ea tells Adapa that in heaven he will be offered the food of death, but he is not to eat of it; also the water of death he will be offered, but he is not to drink of it.

Adapa is brought before Anu and is called to account. He would probably have been condemned. But at the right moment Tammuz and Gizzida interpose on his behalf and plead his cause so successfully that Anu decides not only to let him go unpunished but even to bless him. Anu becomes calm and begins to think matters over. He probably reasons: This man is already half a god; he knows the secrets of heaven and earth; he is in possession of divine wisdom; so why not admit him fully into our circle by conferring immortality upon him? Thereupon he issues the command: "The food of life bring him, that he may eat!" The food of life is brought, but Adapa, mindful of his father's advice, declines to eat; the water of life is brought, but he declines to drink. Anu looks at him and laughs, saying to him: "Come here, Adapa! Why hast thou not eaten, not drunken? Art thou not well? . . . Take him and [bring] him back to his earth!" If Adapa had eaten and had drunk, he would have become one of the lesser gods and would have lived forever. But since he had declined Anu's offer he was sent back to earth and eventually had to die, like all other men. From fragment No. IV it is quite clear, moreover, that, by refusing the food and the water of life, Adapa not only missed immortality but also brought illness and disease upon man. This, together with the statement on fragment No. I that he was a leader among mankind, apparently implies that he was in some way regarded as man's representative. Hence we may conclude that, by refusing to eat and to drink, Adapa missed the chance of gaining immortality for mankind as well.

This, in brief, is the legend of Adapa. Let us now see what deductions we can derive from it for our purposes. First of all, it is clear that this story contains nothing to justify the conclusion that the breaking of the wing of the south wind was the *first* offense ever committed by any human being. Furthermore, it is equally clear that Adapa failed to obtain the priceless boon of immortality not because of any sin or disobedience on his part but because of his strict obedience to the will of Ea, his father, the god of wisdom and the friend of man. And, finally, there is not the slightest trace of any temptation, or any indication whatever that this legend is in any way concerned with the problem of the origin of moral evil. Like the biblical account of the fall of man, the Adapa story wrestles with the questions: "Why must man suffer and die? Why does he not live forever?" But, unlike the biblical account, the answer it gives is not: "Because man has fallen from a state of moral perfection," but rather: "Because Adapa had the chance of gaining immortality for himself and for mankind, but he did not take it. The gift of eternal life was held out to him, but he refused the offer and thus failed of immortality and brought woe and misery upon man." The problem of the origin of sin does not even enter into consideration. Consequently, it is a misnomer to call the Adapa Legend the Babylonian version of the *fall* of man. The Adapa Legend and the biblical story are fundamentally as far apart as the antipodes.

At one time it was rather generally held that the fall of man was depicted on the cylinder seal shown in Figure 17, which pictures two persons seated one on each side of a tree with fruit, toward which both figures stretch out their hands, and between the backs of the two figures the wriggling form of an upright serpent. But this idea has since been abandoned. Both figures, as we can plainly see, are clothed. This alone is in direct contradiction to the biblical story of Paradise, according to which the sense of shame was not awakened in man until after his first transgression, and man was not clothed until he had eaten of the forbidden fruit. This sketch, as Ward[108] has observed, probably represents "two deities of production," a god (the one with the horned headdress) and his divine consort, partaking of the fruit of the date palm, over which they preside; and the serpent, again as Ward has pointed out, is perhaps nothing but the emblem of the goddess without having "any definite relation with the thought of the two figures seated about the palm-tree." A similar view has been given expression by Deimel.[109] It is quite possible that the seal belonged to someone who was engaged in the date industry. But, whatever the correct interpretation of this picture may be, there is no evidence that this scene is at all related to Genesis, chapter 3. Besides, who would think of having the scene of the fall of man engraved on his seal, which was used for commercial purposes?

So far no proof for the *first* sin has been found anywhere in Babylonian or Assyrian literature. If it is at all permissible to speak of a *fall*, it was a fall of the *gods*, not of man. It was the gods who first disturbed the peace of Apsû and Ti᾿âmat; it was Apsû and Mummu who planned the destruction of these gods; it was Ea who, as a measure of self-preservation, killed his ancestor Apsû; and it was Ti᾿âmat and her host who, in a rage of revenge, prepared to bring war and destruction upon the other gods. In Genesis man is created in the image of God; but the Babylonians created their gods in the image of man. The gods not only had human forms and were clothed in garments which differed very little from human dress[110] but also had human needs (requiring food, drink, sleep, etc.) and were guilty of human misconduct, which is something quite different from the anthropomorphisms or human characteristics attributed to God in the Old Testament. The gods were good and the gods were bad, as good and as bad as man. Of the Babylonians can be said what Cicero[111] has said with reference to the poets of Greece and Rome: "The poets have represented the gods as inflamed by anger and maddened by lust, and have displayed to our gaze

---

[108] *Op. cit.*, pp. 138 f.   [109] *Orientalia*, No. 14 (1924), pp. 56 f.

[110] Cf., e.g., Frankfort, *Cylinder Seals*, pp. 22 and 158.

[111] *De natura deorum* i. 16. 42 (translated by H. Rackham in the "Loeb Classical Library").

their wars and battles, their fights and wounds, their hatreds, enmities and quarrels, their births and deaths, their complaints and lamentations, the utter and unbridled license of their passions, their adulteries and imprisonments, their unions with human beings and the birth of mortal progeny from an immortal parent." How could such gods possibly be expected to create something morally perfect? Yes, it was with the blood of such gods that man was created! Since all the gods were evil by nature and since man was formed with their blood, man of course inherited their evil nature. This conclusion is in complete harmony with the following passage from the Babylonian theodicy: "Narru,[112] king from of old, the creator of mankind; gigantic Zulummar,[113] who pinched off their clay[114]; and lady Mama, the queen, who fashioned them, have presented to mankind perverse speech, lies and untruth they presented to them forever."[115] Man, consequently, was *created* evil and was evil from his very beginning. How, then, could he fall? The idea that man fell from a state of moral perfection does not fit into the system or systems of Babylonian speculation.

THE WORD OF THE CREATORS

The efficacy of the almighty word of the Creator in Genesis, chapter 1, where he creates the universe and all that is therein by his divine fiat, finds a rather vague parallel on Tablet IV:23–26, where Marduk, upon the wish of the gods, tests his power by destroying and restoring a garment at the word of his mouth. But this is the only manifestation of such power in all the Babylonian creation stories; the creators are consistently represented after the manner of men (except that they are endowed with superhuman size and power) who bring things into existence by means of physical work, as the Lord God is portrayed in the second chapter of Genesis. The word of the Babylonian deities was *not* almighty. Take the word of Marduk. If his word had been omnipotent, he could have destroyed or, at least, quieted Ti'âmat by means of his word, as he had been

---

[112] I.e., Enlil.   [113] I.e., Ea.

[114] The clay out of which mankind was made.

[115] See Landsberger in *Zeitschrift für Assyriologie*, XLIII (1936), 70 f.

requested by Anshar (Tablet II:117).[116] But the word of the Creator in the opening chapter of Genesis *is* almighty. He commands, and the result is in perfect conformity with his command, or, in the words of Ps. 33:9: "He spoke, and it was; He commanded, and it stood fast." God creates with the same ease with which a superior issues a command to his subordinate.[117]

DIVINE REST

Upon the completion of the universe follows rest. *Enûma elish* devotes almost two full tablets to it. After Marduk has created the universe and mankind and has issued his decrees to the gods, the Anunnaki build Esagila, the temple of Marduk with its stagetower. Thereupon all the gods assemble therein and celebrate. The high point of this celebration is the proclamation of Marduk's fifty names. This act forms, at the same time, the culminating point of the entire epic, for it signifies that Marduk possesses all the power of the great multitude of Babylonian gods and that he is indeed entitled to be the head of the pantheon. Now the chief aim of the entire poem (viz., to justify Marduk's claim to supremacy among the Babylonian gods) has been attained. In comparison with this, the creation of man is of rather secondary importance; it merely serves the purpose of satisfying the discontented gods, as we have seen, and of further enhancing Marduk's glory. What a different impression Gen. 1:1—2:3 makes on us! Here not a trace is found of any proclamation of divine names or of any hymn in divine praise. Here the culminating point is the creation of man, as pointed out above. And as for the rest which his Maker enjoyed, it is described in two short verses: "And on the seventh day God declared His work finished[118] which He had made, and He rested on the

[116] Kramer, in the *Journal of Cuneiform Studies*, II (1948), 47, n. 14, goes beyond the evidence in his declaration: "All that the creating deity [of Babylonia] had to do was to lay his plans, utter the word, and it came to be." The evidence which Kramer invokes is far too meager to prove his point.

[117] For a general study on the efficacy of the divine word see Lorenz Dürr, "Die Wertung des göttlichen Wortes im Alten Testament und im antiken Orient" in *Mitteilungen der Vorderasiatischen Gesellschaft*, Vol. XLII, Heft 1 (1938).

[118] As appears from the two preceding verses, showing that God had already completed his work on the sixth day, we have here a declarative *pi'el* (see König, *Die Genesis*, p. 163; and *Gesenius' Hebrew Grammar*, sec. 52, *g*).

seventh day from all His work which He had made. And God blessed the seventh day and sanctified it; for on it He rested from all His work, in doing which God had brought about creation" (Gen. 2:2 f.).

THE SEVEN TABLETS AND THE SEVEN DAYS

The existence of the seven days in the Hebrew narrative has been traced to the influence of the seven creation tablets. But that is lacking all evidence. To attribute the number seven in Gen. 1:1—2:3 to the fact that *Enûma elish* is composed of seven tablets would be like the attempt, actually made, to establish a relation between the twelve sons of Jacob and the twelve months of the year. In the Genesis account acts of creation were performed on all of the first six days, and on the seventh day God rested; while in *Enûma elish* Tablets II, III, and most of I and IV do not deal with any part of creation, and the story of Marduk's rest begins as early as the first half of Tablet VI and then extends over virtually all of Tablet VII.

THE OUTLINES OF "ENÛMA ELISH" AND GEN. 1:1—2:3

A final and very significant point of comparison is that of the outlines of *Enûma elish* and Gen. 1:1—2:3. Compare:

"ENÛMA ELISH"

1. Apsû and Tiʾâmat and the birth of the first gods
2. The conflict between Ea and Apsû
3. The birth and growth of Marduk
4. The conflict between Marduk and Tiʾâmat
5. Marduk's work of creation
   a) The creation of the firmament
   b) The creation of dry land
   c) The creation of the luminaries
   d) The creation of man
6. The building and dedication of Esagila
7. The hymn to Marduk
8. The epilogue

GENESIS

1. The creation of matter and the formation of heaven and earth in a rude state, the creation of light and the separation of light and darkness
2. The creation of the firmament and the dividing of the waters

3. The creation of dry land, the sea, and plant life
4. The creation of the luminaries
5. The creation of the creatures of the sea and the fowl of the air
6. The creation of the land animals and of man; God blesses man and gives him his instructions
7. God rests from all his work and sanctifies the seventh day

From these two brief outlines it is apparent that each version displays a number of features which are not found in the other. *Enûma elish,* on the one hand, contains an account of the birth of the gods and the various conflicts between them, the building and dedication of a temple complex, and a hymn in honor of the creator. Of this, Genesis says nothing. The biblical account, on the other hand, speaks of a separation of light and darkness, of the creation of plant and animal life, of a charge given to man, and of a blessing bestowed on him. Of this, *Enûma elish* makes no mention.

But the order in which the points of contact follow upon one another is the same. This can perhaps best be brought out by means of the following diagram, drawn up on the basis of the above outlines and in the light of our discussion of the analogies between *Enûma elish* and Genesis.

Enûma elish	Genesis
Divine spirit and cosmic matter are coexistent and coeternal	Divine spirit creates cosmic matter and exists independently of it
Primeval chaos; Ti'âmat enveloped in darkness	The earth a desolate waste, with darkness covering the deep (*těhôm*)
Light emanating from the gods[119]	Light created
The creation of the firmament	The creation of the firmament
The creation of dry land	The creation of dry land
The creation of the luminaries	The creation of the luminaries
The creation of man	The creation of man
The gods rest and celebrate	God rests and sanctifies the seventh day

[119] This light probably emanated from the beginning; but it is not alluded to until somewhat later in the account.

"ENÛMA ELISH" AND GEN. 1:1—2:3 DOUBTLESS
RELATED: THREE EXPLANATIONS

Our examination of the various points of comparison between *Enûma elish* and Gen. 1:1—2:3 shows quite plainly that the similarities are really not so striking as we might expect, considering how closely the Hebrews and the Babylonians were related. In fact, the divergences are much more far-reaching and significant than are the resemblances, most of which are not any closer than what we should expect to find in any two more or less complete creation versions (since both would have to account for the same phenomena and since human minds think along much the same lines) which might come from entirely different parts of the world and which might be utterly unrelated to each other. But the identical sequence of events as far as the points of contact are concerned is indeed remarkable. This can hardly be accidental, since the order could have been different; thus the luminary bodies could have been created immediately after the formation of the sky. There no doubt is a genetic relation between the two stories. But, if so, what is the degree of relationship? Three main possibilities have been suggested: first, the Babylonians borrowed from the Hebrew account; second, the Hebrews borrowed from the Babylonian; third, the two stories revert to a common fountainhead.

THE FIRST EXPLANATION

The first explanation is not very likely, for the Babylonian version antedates the Hebrew account. We cannot determine with certainty to what period *Enûma elish* dates back, but, as we have seen, there are good reasons for placing the date of its composition somewhere between 1894 and 1595 B.C.; moreover, certain strands of this myth undoubtedly go back far into Sumerian times. Since we cannot tell definitely when *Enûma elish* was composed, however, and since priority of publication does not imply priority of existence, this argument must be used with a certain amount of caution. The Hebrew story may have been current in some form or other many centuries before it assumed its present form.

A closely allied theory, designed to account for the similarities between *Enûma elish* and Gen. 1:1—2:3, was developed by Clay.[120] He contended that *Enûma elish* was an amalgamation of a Semitic myth coming from a region called Amurru (i.e., northwestern Mesopotamia, Syria, and Palestine) and a Sumerian myth presumably from the city of Eridu and that the elements which *Enûma elish* and Gen. 1:1—2:3 have in common were importations from Amurru, which, he concluded, were carried to Babylonia by Western Semites emigrating to that land.[121] It is generally recognized, however, that Clay's arguments, resting chiefly on his interpretation of proper names occurring in *Enûma elish*, on migrations (again relying on proper names to carry his point), and on climatic conditions,[122] are based on premises too meager to be conclusive. Clay's idea would, of course, have much more to recommend it if it were possible to prove his thesis that Amurru was the home of the Northern Semites. But, as Poebel[123] and Ungnad[124] have observed, the only way in which this could be done successfully would be on the basis of historical information to that effect or on the basis of uninscribed archeological remains; to date, however, no such evidence has been found to establish Clay's contention. And, even if we had such evidence, it still would not necessarily follow that *Enûma elish* goes back to Western sources; for we still would have to reckon with the possibility that it may have arisen in Babylonia, where the incoming Amorites could have adopted it in a modified form, substituting, for example, some of their own deities for certain ones of the original, just as the Assyrian version of *Enûma elish* substitutes a number of

[120] For a detailed presentation of his arguments see his works: *Amurru, the Home of the Northern Semites* (Philadelphia, 1909), *The Empire of the Amorites* (New Haven, 1919), *A Hebrew Deluge Story in Cuneiform* (New Haven, 1922), and *The Origin of Biblical Traditions* (New Haven, 1923).

[121] See esp. *Amurru, the Home of the Northern Semites*, pp. 53 f.

[122] See *The Origin of Biblical Traditions*, pp. 66–107.

[123] *Orientalistische Literaturzeitung*, Vol. XXIV (1921), cols, 270–72.

[124] *Zeitschrift für Assyriologie*, XXXIV (1922), 19–23. On p. 31 of *The Origin of Biblical Traditions*, Clay maintains that Ungnad, in his brochure *Die ältesten Völkerwanderungen Vorderasiens* (Breslau, 1923), now fully concurs in his view that "the Semitic Babylonians came from Amurru." However, an examination of Ungnad's pamphlet (particularly p. 5) shows quite definitely that Ungnad is not so positive on this point as Clay's assertion would lead one to believe.

divinities for those of the Babylonian version, and that from Babylonia, moreover, it might then have spread to the Westland.

The second view, viz., that certain features of Gen. 1:1—2:3 are due to influences emanating from Babylonia, has enjoyed widespread popularity among scholars ever since the discovery of the Babylonian creation tablets. The main arguments that can be advanced in favor of this position are the remarkably close relationship between the biblical and the Babylonian stories of the flood,[125] and the fact that for some time during the second millennium B.C. the Babylonian script, language, and literature to a certain degree pervaded the Westland.

By approximately 1800 B.C. Babylonian writing had traveled as far west as Cappadocia, via Assyria. From about the fourteenth or fifteenth century B.C. we have numerous documents composed in Babylonian and discovered among the ruins of the ancient Hittite capital, Hattusas (near modern Boghazköy), in Asia Minor. Among these are quite a number of fragments of Sumerian-Babylonian-Hittite vocabularies and several fragments of the Gilgamesh Epic. One of the fragments of the Gilgamesh Epic is written in Babylonian, about a dozen of them are written in Hittite, and a number of other pieces are in Hurrian (or Horite). During the same period we find that Babylonian has become the diplomatic language of southwestern Asia and Egypt, so that the correspondence between the princes of Syria, Phoenicia, and Palestine and their Egyptian overlords was carried on in the writing and language not of Egypt but of Babylonia, as we can see from the more than three hundred cuneiform clay tablets unearthed at Tell el-Amarna, a village in Upper Egypt. This latter observation, in particular, points to close relations between Babylonia and the West for over a longer period of time, for no language can gain such extraordinary importance overnight. What these relations were which made Babylonian the language of diplomacy we cannot tell with certainty. At first thought one might be inclined to attribute this phenomenon to Babylonian invasions. However, the

---

[125] See the writer's book *The Gilgamesh Epic and Old Testament Parallels*, esp. pp. 224–69.

Babylonian invasions of the Westland before the Amarna period were few and of short duration; they alone could hardly have established Babylonian as the language of international communication throughout southwestern Asia. This remarkable circumstance was no doubt brought about through the medium of Babylonian trade, for which we have a bit of Old Testament evidence in Josh. 7:21, where reference is made to "a beautiful mantle from Shinar."

Furthermore, in order to learn the writing and the language of the Babylonians, it was of course necessary to study their literature. For this purpose, however, texts were required. And so texts were introduced. This is evident from the fact that among the tablets discovered at Tell el-Amarna were found copies, in the form of school exercises, of the Babylonian stories of Ereshkigal, the queen of the underworld, and of Adapa, who was misled into refusing the bread of life and the water of life.[126] All this, however, meant not only learning the Babylonian language but also exposing the mind to Babylonian thought and speculation.

On the basis of these considerations it is not unreasonable to assume that some of the Babylonian traditions, such as the stories of creation and of the deluge, were known also to the Hebrews, at least to their leaders. As a matter of fact, in view of the sequence in which the points of contact follow upon one another in *Enûma elish* and in Gen. 1:1—2:3, one is tempted to conclude that not only was the main Babylonian creation story known to the Hebrews but that some of this material was actually used in the composition of the biblical account.

But this way of explaining the relationship between the two accounts has received vigorous opposition ever since it was proposed. Some object to it because they hold that it would bring the date of Genesis down too far. Others reject it because they feel that a dependence of Genesis upon *Enûma elish* would be inconsistent with the integrity of the sacred writers and incompatible with the scriptural doctrine of inspiration.

In the first place, however, we need not assume, as was for-

[126] J. A. Knudtzon, *Die El-Amarna-Tafeln* (Leipzig, 1915), Part I; Zimmern in Gunkel, *Schöpfung und Chaos . . . .*, pp. 150 f.; and A. T. Olmstead, *History of Palestine and Syria* (New York and London, 1931), p. 148.

134   THE BABYLONIAN GENESIS

merly done, that the Hebrews first became acquainted with Babylonian traditions during the Exile (sixth century B.C.), when they had the life and civilization of their captors immediately before them and could not help but be exposed to their ideas. For the portions of the myths of Ereshkigal and of Adapa which have been recovered among the Tell el-Amarna tablets in Egypt plainly show that Babylonian traditions had reached Palestine and had traveled as far south as Egypt even before the Hebrews crossed the Jordan. Some of these stories may have found their way into Canaan and Egypt and have become the intellectual possession of a certain percentage of the population long before the Exodus. Some of the more learned among the Hebrews, who were not *all* slaves, may have become familiar with Babylonian literature while they were in Egypt.[127]

In the second place, in those times it was natural and customary to borrow without acknowledgment. What little value the Babylonians attached to authorship is evident, for example, from the fact that hardly any of the authors of the Babylonian poetic compositions are known. As for the Old Testament, one prophet quotes or paraphrases the words of another without any indication of his source (cf. Jer. 48:5 with Isa. 15:5; Jer. 49:14–16 with Obad. 1–4; Joel 3:16 with Amos 1:2; Mic. 4:1–5 with Isa. 2:2–5; etc.). And when the Old Testament writers do refer to sources which they apparently consulted, such as the Book of the Chronicles of the Kings of Israel, the Book of the Chronicles of the Kings of Judah, and the Book of the Kings of Judah and Israel, it is done primarily—if not exclusively—for the purpose of supplying the student of Hebrew history with additional references, not for the purpose of acknowledging indebtedness. This can be seen quite clearly from the ever recurring statement:

[127] Some scholars have gone back even further, viz., to the time of Abraham (*ca.* 2000 B.C.), and have suggested that Abraham, as a native of Babylonia (Gen. 11:27 ff.) and as one who had formerly served the idols (Josh. 24:2), like his fellow-citizens may have learned this Babylonian creation story, and that, upon migrating from Babylonia to Canaan, he may have brought these cosmological traditions along and passed them on to the next generation. While the evidence making such an assumption a definite possibility is multiplying (cf. G. E. Wright in *The Biblical Archaeologist*, X [1947], 12), there is as yet no proof for this explanation.

"Now the *rest* of the acts of [So-and-so] and all that he did, are they not written in the Book of the Chronicles of the Kings of Israel?" (or "Judah," as the case may be);[128] or, "Now the *rest* of the acts of [So-and-so]; behold, they are written in the Book of the Kings of Judah and Israel."[129] Moreover, if we concede, for the sake of argument, that the creation account in Gen. 1:1—2:3 rests to some extent upon the Babylonian, what in the final analysis does it contain that deserves acknowledgment? How much of this story could one confidently trace to *Enûma elish*, if anything at all? If Gen. 1:1—2:3 really was influenced by *Enûma elish*, then it is reasonably certain that at least the following elements go back to the Babylonian epic: (1) *part* of the outline; (2) the conception of an immense primeval body of water containing the component parts of the earth; (3) the idea that the creation of the firmament was attended by a separation of the primeval waters; and (4) the existence of light before the luminaries. But even in these few points we have no complete correspondence between *Enûma elish* and Genesis; in fact, even here the differences far outweigh the similarities. If it were possible to establish definitely that the biblical account was dependent upon the Babylonian, we could, of course, conclude that in all probability some of the other ideas, in addition to those just mentioned, also went back to *Enûma elish*. But it would be impossible to say with any degree of certainty *which* of these other ideas were taken over from the Babylonian version, since they were all rather widely diffused in ancient times and therefore could easily have been derived from sources other than *Enûma elish*. Such an idea, for example, is the conception of a primeval darkness.[130]

In the third place, the doctrine of inspiration is, of course, indisputably taught in Scripture; we need only recall the ever

128 See I Kings 15:31, 16:5, 22:39; II Kings 1:18, 14:28, 15:6, 16:19, 20:20, etc.

129 See II Chron. 32:32, 35:26 f., 36:8. In the same way we must probably interpret also I Chron. 29:29 f.; II Chron. 12:15, 16:11, 24:27.

130 For a general treatment of the metamorphoses which myths and legends undergo as they travel from one place to another and of the difficulties connected with tracing the various strands back to their sources see Wundt, *Völkerpsychologie*, II, Part 3 (Leipzig, 1909), 500–552, and Lukas, *op. cit.*, pp. 255–65.

recurring Old Testament phrase, "Thus saith the Lord," and such New Testament passages as "All Scripture is given by inspiration of God" (II Tim. 3:16); "No prophecy ever originated in the will of man, but holy men of God spoke as they were moved by the Holy Ghost" (II Pet. 1:21); and "When ye received the word of God which ye heard of us, ye accepted it not as the word of men but, as it is in truth, as the word of God" (I Thess. 2:13). However, this does not imply that the sacred writers were exempt from all studies and investigations. On the contrary, we have just seen that the authors of the books of Kings and Chronicles consulted the archives of the land. And the author of the Third Gospel says very distinctly that he made a thorough study of the life of Christ before writing his account, for he tells us: "Inasmuch as many have undertaken to draw up a narrative concerning the things which have taken place among us, as they handed it down to us who were eyewitnesses from the beginning and who became ministers of the word, it seemed good to me also, *having carefully investigated it all from the beginning,* to write thee, most excellent Theophilus, a connected account of it" (Luke 1:1–3). It is true that the biblical writers make mention only of having utilized *native* sources. They nowhere state that they ever drew upon *foreign,* or *heathen,* material; but they do not deny it either.[131] And why could they not have studied foreign literature and then have incorporated in their own writings some of the elements of this material that were true or were suited to illustrate truth (cf. p. 111)? The late Professor Franz Pieper,[132] of Concordia Theological Seminary (St. Louis, Missouri), one of the most conservative Protestant institutions in the world, has solved the problem involved in this connection as follows:

As the Holy Ghost employed the style which He *found* in the individual writers, thus He also utilized the historical knowledge which the writers al-

[131] I pass over Ezra 1:2–4, 4:11–22, 5:6–17, 6:1–12, 7:11–26; Neh. 6:5–7, containing letters to or from the kings of Persia, and similar material. I pass over also Acts 17:28, I Cor. 15:33, and Titus 1:12 because the quotations which they contain were obviously embodied therein for the purpose of meeting the Greeks on their own ground.

[132] *Christliche Dogmatik,* I (St. Louis, 1924), 284 f. The following quotation is a translation from the German original.

ready possessed either through their own experience, or through their own investigations, or through communications received from other persons. The
example of the first Pentecost brings this out very clearly. Of the resurrection
of Christ the apostles had knowledge through their own experience before
Pentecost. Yet on the first Pentecost they spoke, as of the other mighty deeds
of God, so also of the resurrection of Christ, "as the Spirit gave them utterance."

Another dogmatician of the same institution, Professor John T.
Mueller,[133] makes the following declaration:

Independent study and historical research were indeed carried on at times
by the holy writers; for they themselves tell us that they were prompted to
write not only new revelations, but also such things as they knew in consequence of their general study and their special experience, Gal. 1, 17–24;
Luke 1, 1 ff. However, this fact does not disprove the doctrine of inspiration,
since the Holy Spirit utilized for His beneficent purpose of giving to fallen
man the Word of God also the general knowledge of the sacred penmen, just
as He utilized their natural gifts and talents (experience, style, culture, etc.).
Inspiration is not mere revelation, but the divine prompting (*impulsus scri-
bendi*) to record the truths which God desired that men should know in words
He Himself supplied, 2 Sam. 23, 2 ff. Some of these truths were given the holy
writers by direct revelation, 1 Cor. 11, 23; 14, 37; 2, 7–13; others were known
to them by experience, Acts 17, 28; Gal. 2, 11–14; others, again, by direct in-
vestigation and special research, Luke 1, 1 ff. In the treatment of the doctrine
of divine inspiration the question is not: "How did the holy writers obtain the
truths which they wrote?" but rather: "Did the Holy Ghost prompt the
sacred writers to write down certain words and thoughts which God wanted
men to know?" The fact that this was actually the case is clearly taught in
Holy Scripture, 2 Tim. 3, 16; 2 Pet. 1, 21, so that the doctrine of inspiration
is beyond dispute.

We have, moreover, good reasons for believing that at least
some of the authors of the Old Testament *were* acquainted with
foreign literature and that in certain cases and to a certain degree they actually made use of it in the composition of their
own books. For example, in connection with the Marduk-
Tiᵓâmat conflict we quoted the following lines from an inscription excavated at Ras Shamra:

> When thou shalt smite Lôtan, the fleeing serpent,
> (And) shalt put an end to the tortuous serpent,
> Shalyaṭ of the seven heads. . . . .

[133] *Christian Dogmatics* (St. Louis, 1934), p. 110.

This passage, as we have indicated above, influenced Ps. 74:4, referring to "the *heads* of Leviathan," and Isa. 27:1:

> On that day the Lord will punish
> With His sword, which is hard and great and strong,
> Leviathan, the fleeing serpent,
> And Leviathan, the tortuous serpent,
> And He will slay the crocodile that is in the sea.

To this passage from Ras Shamra we can add another one from the same place which also has left its marks on biblical literature:

> Behold, thine enemies, O Baal;
> Behold, thine enemies thou shalt smite.
> Behold, thou shalt destroy thine adversaries![134]

These lines remind us rather forcefully of Ps. 92:10:

> For, behold, Thine enemies, O Lord,
> For, behold, Thine enemies shall perish!
> All the workers of iniquity shall be scattered!

Hardly anyone will deny that in these three biblical passages the sacred writers took over figures of speech derived from foreign literature and that they patterned their lines after those from Ras Shamra, just as certain of the classical writers of the Christian Era patterned some of their finest literary productions after Greek and Roman masterpieces. Since the Old Testament was intended also for the gentile world, it is but natural that the biblical authors availed themselves of figures of speech and imagery with which also Israel's neighbors were familiar, or which were at least easily understandable to them. It may be added, however, that identical phraseology does not necessarily imply identical theology.

Considering all this, I personally fail to see why it should be incompatible with the doctrine of inspiration to assume that Gen. 1:1—2:3 might in a measure be dependent on *Enûma elish*. But I reject the idea that the biblical account gradually

---

[134] See Virolleaud in *Syria. . . .* , Vol. XVI (1935), Pl. XI: 8 f. With the translation cf. Gordon, *Ugaritic Handbook*, p. 113, or the same author's book *The Loves and Wars of Baal and Anat* (Princeton and London, 1943), p. 20; and H. L. Ginsberg in *The Biblical Archaeologist*, VIII (1945), 54. These lines have been rendered somewhat differently by J. Obermann, *Ugaritic Mythology* (New Haven, 1948), p. 71.

evolved out of the Babylonian; for that the differences are far too great and the similarities far too insignificant. In the light of the differences, the resemblances fade away almost like the stars before the sun.

THE THIRD EXPLANATION

There is, however, yet another way of accounting for the similarities between Genesis and *Enûma elish*, viz., both versions may have sprung from a common source of some kind. One of the most recent advocates of this view was the late Professor Ira M. Price of the University of Chicago, who attributed the common elements to a common inheritance of man going back to "a time when the human race occupied a common home and held a common faith."[135]

CONCLUDING REMARKS

There are those who seem to be convinced that Gen. 1:1—2:3 shows Babylonian traces, while others appear to be just as convinced that it does not. In my estimation, no incontrovertible evidence can for the present be produced for either side; I believe that *the whole question must still be left open.* But whatever the true facts of the case may be, whether the biblical account is or is not dependent on Babylonian material, there is no reason, as we have seen, why anyone should be disturbed in his mind and lose his reverence for the opening chapter of the Bible. If certain features of the biblical account *were* derived from the Babylonian, this was done in conformity with the will of Him who according to Heb. 1:1 revealed Himself "in divers manners." Moreover, a comparison of the Babylonian creation story with the first chapter of Genesis makes the sublime character of the latter stand out in even bolder relief. *Enûma elish* refers to a multitude of divinities emanating from the elementary world-matter; the universe has its origin in the generation of numerous gods and goddesses personifying cosmic spaces or forces in nature, and in the orderly and purposeful arrangement of pre-existent matter; the world is not *created* in the biblical sense of the term but *fashioned* after the manner of human craftsmen; as for man, he is created with the blood of a deity that might well

[135] *The Monuments and the Old Testament* (Philadelphia, etc., 1925), pp. 129 f.

be called a devil among the gods, and the sphere of activity assigned to man is the service of the gods. In Gen. 1:1—2:3, on the other hand, there stands at the very beginning *one* God, who is not co-united and coexistent with an eternal world-matter and who does not first develop Himself into a series of separate deities but who creates matter out of nothing and exists independently of all cosmic matter and remains *one* God to the end. Here the world is created by the sovereign *word* of God, without recourse to all sorts of external means. God speaks, and it is done; he commands, and it stands fast. Add to this the doctrine that man was created in the image of a holy and righteous God, to be the lord of the earth, the air, and the sea, and we have a number of differences between *Enûma elish* and Gen. 1:1—2:3 that make all similarities shrink into utter insignificance.[136] These exalted conceptions in the biblical account of creation give it a depth and dignity unparalleled in any cosmogony known to us from Babylonia or Assyria.

[136] Cf. Skinner, *op. cit.*, pp. 6 f.; A. Dillmann, *Genesis*, trans. W. B. Stevenson, I (Edinburgh, 1897), 43.

APPENDIX

THE following texts are not creation stories at all. Nevertheless, they are added here because they enter into consideration in chapter iii. The first two of them, moreover, bear some very striking resemblances to the Marduk-Tiᵃ̈mat fight in *Enûma elish*.

THE SLAYING OF THE "LABBU"[1]

The legend which we are about to consider tells of the slaying of a monster called *labbu*.[2] This word means "lion." However, in the course of the story the same creature is also called a serpent. We may therefore conclude that it was a composite monster or dragon with leonine and serpentine attributes. The fight with this creature, as King[3] has correctly pointed out, took place not *before* but *after* the creation of the world, after man had already been created and cities had already been built. In fact, as King further states, men and gods alike were terror-stricken at the appearance of this monster, and it was for the express purpose of delivering "the wide land" from this dragon that one of the gods finally went out and slew it. The legend runs as follows:

OBVERSE

1. The cities sighed, the people . [. . . .],
2. The people decreased in number . [. . . .];
3. For their lamentation there was none [to . . . .],
4. For their cry there was none [to . . . .].

---

[1] Text published by L. W. King in *Cuneiform Texts from Babylonian Tablets, etc., in the British Museum*, Vol. XIII (London, 1901), Pls. 33 f., and translated by him in *The Seven Tablets of Creation* (London, 1902), I, 116–21; P. Jensen, *Assyrisch-babylonische Mythen und Epen* (Berlin, 1900), pp. 44–47; Erich Ebeling in Hugo Gressmann, *Altorientalische Texte zum Alten Testament* (Berlin and Leipzig, 1926), pp. 138 f.; and others.

[2] Formerly this term was read also as *ribbu* and was then equated with the biblical *Rahab*. But that reading cannot be authenticated. The reading *labbu*, on the other hand, is now well established (see Fr. Hrozný in *Mitteilungen der Vorderasiatischen Gesellschaft*, VIII, Heft 5 [1903], 107; and Fr. Nötscher, *Ellil in Sumer und Akkad* [Hannover, 1927], p. 58).

[3] *Babylonian Religion and Mythology* (London and New York, 1899), p. 84, and *The Seven Tablets of Creation*, I, 116, n. 1.

5. "Who [brought forth] the serpent(-dragon)?"
6. "The sea [brought forth] the serpent(-dragon)."
7. Enlil drew a picture of [the dragon] in the sky:[4]
8. "(A stretch of) fifty double-hours[5] is his length (and of) one double-hour [his height],
9. Six cubits his mouth, twelve cubits [his . . . .],
10. Twelve cubits is the circumference of [his] ea[rs];
11. At (a distance of) sixty cubits he [can snatch(?)] the birds;
12. In the water nine cubits deep he drags;
13. He raises his tail [. . . .]."
14. All the gods of heaven [. . . .].
15. In heaven the gods lay prostrate before [Sin][6]
16. And hast[ily(?) grasped] the robe of Sin:
17. "Who will go and [slay] the *labbu*,
18. (And) will deli[ver] the wide land,
19. And exercise kingship [over all(?)]?"[7]
20. "Go, Tishpak, s[lay] the *labbu*,
21. [And so] deliver the wide land [from him(?)],
22. And exercise kingship [over all(?)]!"
23. "Thou hast sent me, O Lord, [to slay(?)] the creature[8] of the river;
24. But I do not know the [. . . .] of the *labbu*."

The last line seems to indicate that Tishpak declined to go to battle against the dragon. On the analogy of *Enûma elish* and the myth of the Zû-bird, we are probably justified in concluding that, even if Tishpak accepted, he failed in his mission and that at long last some *other* god came forward and slew the monster and then was accorded the highest rank among the gods. Who this god was we have no means of knowing, but in all probability it was not Tishpak.

    [4] The lamentation reaches Enlil, who then draws a picture of the monster to make the gods realize the dragon's frightful nature. This line is probably to account for the existence of the Milky Way.

    [5] The term "double-hour" denotes the distance which can be covered in two hours' traveling, i.e., about seven miles.

    [6] The moon-god.

    [7] In ll. 17–19 the gods appeal to Sin; in ll. 20–22 Sin addresses Tishpak; and ll. 23 ff. contain Tishpak's answer to Sin.

    [8] Reading *ri-ḫu-ut*.

Except for a few traces the rest of the obverse and the beginning of the reverse of this tablet are destroyed. When the text again becomes legible, we find ourselves in the midst of a battle scene.

REVERSE

1. [. . . .] he opened his mouth and [spoke] to god [. . . .]:
2. "Stir up the clouds (and) [create(?)] a storm;
3. The seal of thy life [thou shalt hold(?)] before thy face;[9]
4. Shoot off (an arrow) and sl[ay] the *labbu* [. . . .]!"
5. He stirred up clouds (and) [created(?)] a storm,
6. The seal of his life [he held(?)] before his face,
7. He shot off (an arrow) and [slew] the *labbu* [. . . .].
8. For three years (and) three months, one day and a [night]
9. The blood of the *labbu* flowed [. . . .].

Another version of this myth has been recovered at Ashur, the old capital of Assyria.[10] Column i of the tablet on which this version is recorded is completely destroyed, with the exception of a few signs; and the first twenty lines of column ii are of rather uncertain meaning, owing to the defective condition of the text. The rest of the second column reads as follows:

21. In the sea the serpent(-dragon) was created . [. . . .].
22. [His] back was sixty double-hours long.
23. [His he]ad was thirty double-hours high.
24. [His] eyelids extended over (an area of) half (a double-hour) each.
25. [His feet] are accustomed to take steps twenty double-hours long.
26. He ate fish, the creatures of [the sea];
27. He ate birds, the creatures of [the sky];
28. He ate wild asses, the creatures of [the steppe];
29. [He ate] people, to/for the people [. . . .].

(*The rest is too fragmentary for connected translation*)

[9] As a talisman.
[10] Text published by Ebeling, *Keilschrifttexte aus Assur religiösen Inhalts*, No. 6, and translated by the same author in *Orientalistische Literaturzeitung*, Vol. XIX (1916), cols. 106–8, and by King, *Legends of Babylon and Egypt in Relation to Hebrew Tradition* (London, 1918), pp. 117 f.

THE MYTH OF THE STORM-GOD ZÛ[11]

This story is similar in character to the foregoing one. It has come down to us in two redactions—the Ninevite and the Susan. In this book we shall follow the Ninevite version, using the Susan fragments merely for the purpose of filling in gaps. Column i of the legend is destroyed almost entirely. Column ii begins with the end of a sentence from the previous column and reads as follows:

1. Also the omens of all the gods he contro[lled].
2. ⌜. . . .⌝ he sent Zû;
3. ⌜. . . .⌝ like ⌜. . . .⌝ Enlil entrusted to him.
4. Pure ⌜. . . .⌝ water before him.
5. His eyes behold what Enlil does as sovereign.[12]
6. The crown of his sovereignty, the robe of his divinity,
7. The tablet of destinies (belonging to) his ⌜divinity(?)⌝ Zû beholds again and again.
8. And as he beholds again and again the father of the gods, the god of Duranki,[13]
9. He conceives in his heart a desire(?) for Enlil's position;
10. As Zû beholds again and again the father of the gods, the god of Duranki,
11. He conceives in his heart a desire(?) for Enlil's position.
12. "I will take the tablet of the destinies of the gods, even I!
13. Also the omens of all the gods I will control!
14. I will establish (my) throne and will control(?) the decrees!
15. I will control all the Igigi together!"
16. After his heart has planned the attack,
17. He waits for the beginning of the day at the entrance of (Enlil's) chamber, which he had beheld repeatedly.

[11] The Ninevite recension has been published by King in *Cuneiform Texts.* . . . , Vol. XV (London, 1902), Pls. 39 f., and translated by Jensen, *op. cit.*, pp. 46–53, and by Ebeling in Gressmann, *op. cit.*, pp. 141–43. The Susan material has been published and translated by V. Scheil in *Revue d'assyriologie*, XXXV (1938), 14–25.

[12] *Lit.*: His eyes behold the exercise of Enlilship.

[13] "God of Duranki" is an epithet of Enlil. Duranki (meaning "the bond of heaven and earth") was the name of the stagetower of Enlil's temple in the city of Nippur.

18. As Enlil was washing in clear water,
19. After his tiara had been taken off and placed on the throne,
20. He seized the tablet of destinies with [his] hand
21. And usurped sovereignty, (the power) to issue decrees.
22. Zû (then) flew away and [hid(?)] in his mountain.
23. Numbness was poured out, silence prevailed.
24. Enlil, the father (of the gods), their counsellor, was be-numbed (with fear).
25. The sanctuary was deprived of its fear-inspiring splendor.
26. The gods of the land turned hither and thither for counsel.
27. Anu[14] opened his mouth and said,
28. Speaking to the gods, his children:
29. "Let that god there[15] slay Zû
30. And make his name great in the inhabited places!"
31. The prince they called, the son of Anu.
32. The commander speaks to him.
33. [Ada]d,[16] the prince, they called, the son of Anu.
34. [The comm]ander speaks to him:
35. "[Thou migh]ty, victorious Adad, may thine onslaught be not repelled.
36. With thy weapon cause lightning to strike[17] Zû,
37. [And thy name] shall be (the) great(est) in the assembly of the great gods.
38. [Among the go]ds thy brothers thou shalt have no equal.
39. Shrines [shall come into existence and] be built (for thee).
40. [In] the four [regions of the world] establish thy cult places.
41. [Thy cult places] shall enter Ekur.[18]
42. [Be thou mighty] in the presence of the gods, and powerful be thy name!"
43. [Adad] replied concerning (this) commission,
44. Speaking a word [to Anu], his father:

[14] Anu, the god of heaven and originally the highest god, presides at this meeting.

[15] Reading *i-lu-ma an-nu-um* (Susan recension).

[16] The storm-god par excellence.

[17] Reading *shu-ub-ri-iq* (Susan recension).

[18] Enlil's temple at Nippur. Adad shall occupy Enlil's place in Ekur.

45. "[My father], who shall set out for the inaccessible [mountain]?
46. [Who is li]ke Zû among the gods, thy children?
47. [The tablet of destinies] he has seized with his hand,
48. He has usurped [sovereignty], (the power) to issue decrees;
49. [Zû has] flown away and has hid(?) in his mountain.
50. [. . . . the word of] his mouth is like (that of) the god, the god of Duranki.
51. [The one who opp]oses (him) becomes like clay.
52. [At the sight of hi]m the gods droop(?)."
53. [(Thereupon) Anu] told (him) not to go on the road.

(Remainder of the column broken away)

COLUMN III

The beginning of this column is almost completely destroyed. However, enough is left to show very clearly that some other divinity is called upon to set out against Zû and to recover the tablet of destinies. But even this deity shrinks from the task and declines. The story then continues:

7. ⌜Shara they called,⌝ the first-born of Ishtar.
8. The commander speaks to him:
9. "[Thou mi]ghty, victorious Shara, may thine onslaught be not repelled!
10. [Smite(?)] Zû with thy weapon,
11. [And thy name] shall be (the) great(est) in the assembly of the great gods.
12. [Amo]ng the gods thy brothers thou shalt have no equal.
13. Shrines [shall] come into existence and be built (for thee).
14. In the four regions of the world establish thy cult places.
15. Thy cult places shall enter Ekur.
16. Be thou mighty in the presence of the gods, and powerful be thy name!"
17. Shara replied concerning (this) commission,
18. Speaking a word to Anu, his father:
19. "My father, who shall set out for the inaccessible mountain?
20. Who is like unto Zû among the gods, thy children?

21. The tablet of destinies he has seized with his hand,
22. He has usurped sovereignty, (the power) to issue decrees;
23. Zû has flown away and [hid(?)] in his mountain.
24. ⌈. . . .⌉ the word of [his] mouth is like (that of) the god, the god of [Duranki].
25. [The one who opposes him becomes like clay].
26. [At the sight of him the gods droop(?)]."
27. [(Thereupon) Anu told him not to go on the road].

The rest of the legend is too fragmentary for translation. The story, of course, had a happy ending for the gods. We may assume as a certainty that one of the gods finally recovered the tablet of destinies and thus became the head of the pantheon. According to a hymn, this hero was Marduk, for in it he is called "the one who crushed the skull of Zû."[19] However, we cannot be sure whether that passage refers to the legend in the versions before us (which are essentially alike) or whether it has reference to quite a different, still unknown version of the Zû story.

THE ADAPA LEGEND[20]

The story of Adapa, which we have briefly discussed in the preceding chapter, has been preserved to us on four fragmentary clay tablets. Of these, No. II was found among the archives of the Egyptian kings Amenhotep III and IV (about the first half of the fourteenth century B.C.), while the others have come from the library of the Assyrian king Ashurbanipal (about 668–630 B.C.). Numbers III and IV apparently belong together, since they are

[19] See Johannes Hehn in *Beiträge zur Assyriologie*, V (1906), 309:15.

[20] Cuneiform text of fragment No. I published by Clay, *A Hebrew Deluge Story in Cuneiform* (New Haven, 1922), Pl. IV, with a photograph on Pl. VI; of No. II by Otto Schroeder in *Vorderasiatische Schriftdenkmäler*, Vol. XII (Leipzig, 1915), No. 194; of No. III by S. Langdon, *Sumerian Epic of Paradise, the Flood and the Fall of Man* (Philadelphia, 1915), Pl. IV, 3, and by R. Campbell Thompson, *The Epic of Gilgamish* (Oxford, 1930), Pl. 31 (K. 8743); and of No. IV by S. A. Strong in *Proceedings of the Society of Biblical Archaeology*, XVI (1894), 274 f. For a new collation of No. IV see Langdon, *op. cit.*, pp. 46–48. Translations of these fragments by R. W. Rogers, *Cuneiform Parallels to the Old Testament* (New York and Cincinnati, 1926), pp. 69–76; Clay, *op. cit.*, p. 41; J. A. Knudtzon, *Die El-Amarna-Tafeln* (Leipzig, 1915), Part I, pp. 965–69; Ebeling in Gressmann, *op. cit.*, pp. 143–46; and others.

written in the same hand and have the same clay texture;[21] they contain a variant account of the story told on the first two tablets. All these fragments, except No. I, are inscribed in prose. The myth was used as part of an incantation against illness and disease, as we can see from the closing lines of the last fragment.

FRAGMENT NO. I

1. [Wi]sdom he [possessed(?) . . . .].
2. His command was like the command of [Anu] ⌈. . . .⌉.
3. With wide understanding he[22] had perfected him to expound(?) the decrees of the land.
4. He had given him wisdom, (but) he had not given him eternal life.
5. At that time, in those years, of the wise son of Eridu—
6. Ea had created him as a leader among mankind—
7. Of the wise one, no one treated his command lightly.
8. The skilful, the exceedingly wise among the Anunnaki was he;[23]
9. The pure one, the clean of hands, the temple provisioner, the observer of the rites.
10. With the bakers he does the baking,
11. With the bakers of Eridu he does the baking.
12. Food and water he daily provides for Eridu.
13. With his clean hands he sets the (sacred) table;
14. Without him the table is not cleared.
15. He steers the ship, he does the fishing for Eridu.
16. At that time Adapa of Eridu,
17. The son of Ea, at the time of retiring(?) upon the bed,
18. Daily attended to(?) the lock of (the gate of) Eridu.
19. [At] the bright quay, the Quay of the New Moon, he embarked the sailboat.
20. [The wind b]lew, and his ship glided along.
21. [With the o]ar he steers his ship
22. [. . . . upon] the wide sea.[24]

(Rest destroyed)

---

[21] See Langdon, *op. cit.*, p. 38, n. 2.

[22] Ea, the god of wisdom.　　　　[23] Adapa.

[24] The Persian Gulf, on whose shores Eridu was located.

1. (*Destroyed*)
2. The south wind [blew and submerged him],
3. Plunging [him] into the realm of ⌐Ea⌐.
4. "South wind, ⌐. . . .⌐,
5. Thy wi[ng] will I break!" As he had said with his mouth,
6. The wing of [the sou]th wind was broken. Seven days
7. [The sou]th wind did not blow upon the land. Anu
8. Called [to] Ilabrat, his vizier:
9. "Why has the south wind not blown upon the land for the (last) seven days?"
10. Ilabrat, his vizier, answered him: "My lord,
11. Adapa, the son of Ea, has broken the wing of the south wind."
12. When Anu heard this statement,
13. He cried: "Help!" He arose from his throne (and said): "[Let] them bring him to me!"
14. At this point Ea—(for) he knows the things in heaven—laid hold on [him] and
15. Caused [Adapa] to wear ⌐long hair⌐;[25] [he clothed him]
16. With a mourning garment and gave him counsel,
17. [Saying: "Adapa], thou must go [to Anu, the k]ing;
18. [The road to heaven thou must take. When] thou ascendest to heaven
19. [And approachest the gate of Anu],
20. [Tammuz and Gizzida] will be standing in the gate of Anu.
21. When they see thee, they will ask thee: 'M[an],
22. For whose sake dost thou look thus? Adapa, for whose sake
23. Art thou clad in a mourning garment?' 'From our land two gods have disappeared.
24. Therefore I am made up like this.' 'Who are the two gods who have disappeared from the land?'
25. 'They are Tammuz and Gizzida.' They will look at one another

[25] Bruno Meissner, *Beiträge zum assyrischen Wörterbuch*, I (Chicago, 1931), 52 f.

26. And will smile.[26] Kind words
27. They will speak to Anu (and) the pleasant countenance of Anu
28. They will show thee.[27] As thou standest before Anu,
29. They will offer thee the food of death;
30. Do not eat (it). The water of death they will offer thee;
31. Do not drink (it). A garment they will offer thee;
32. Clothe thyself (with it). Oil they will offer thee; anoint thyself (with it).
33. The instruction which I have given thee do not forget; the words
34. Which I have spoken unto thee, hold fast." The messenger
35. Of Anu arrived: "Adapa has broken
36. The wing of the south wind. Bring him before me!"
37. He made him take [the ro]ad to heaven, and to heaven he ascended.
38. [And] as he ascended to heaven (and) approached the gate of Anu,
39. Tammuz and Gizzida were standing in the gate of Anu.
40. When they saw Adapa, they cried: "Help!
41. Man, for whose sake dost thou look thus? Adapa,
42. For whose sake art thou clad in a mourning garment?"
43. "Two gods have disappeared from the land, and so I am clad in
44. A mourning garment." "Who are the two gods who have disappeared from the land?"
45. "Tammuz and Gizzida." They looked at one another
46. And smiled. When Adapa entered into the presence of Anu, the king,
47. And Anu saw him, he called out:
48. "Come here, Adapa! Why hast thou broken the wing of the south wind?"
49. Adapa answered Anu: "My lord,
50. For the house of my lord I was catching fish on the high sea.
51. The sea was like a mirror(?);

[26] Benno Landsberger in *Zeitschrift für Assyriologie*, XL (1931), 297 f.; XLII (1934), 163–65.

[27] I.e., they will induce Anu to be friendly toward him.

52. (But) the south wind came blowing and submerged me;
53. I was plunged into the realm of my lord. In the wrath of my heart
54. I cursed [the sou]th wind." [Tammuz and] Gizzida
55. Spoke up at his side, saying ⌜kind words⌝
56. To Anu. His heart became calm, he became silent.[28]
57. "Why has Ea revealed to an impure(?) man
58. The heart of heaven and earth?[29]
59. He has made him strong (and) has made him a name.
60. As for us, what shall we do with him? The food of life
61. Bring him, that he may eat." The food of life
62. They brought him, but he did not eat. The water of life
63. They brought him, but he did not drink. A garment
64. They [brou]ght him, and he clothed himself (with it). Oil
65. They brought him, and he anointed himself (with it).
66. Anu looked at him and laughed at him.
67. "Come here, Adapa! Why hast thou not eaten, not drunken?
68. Art thou not well? ⌜. . . .⌝." "Ea, my lord,
69. Said: 'Do not eat, do not drink!' "
70. "Take him and [bring] him back to his earth!"

(Remainder broken away)

FRAGMENT NO. III[30]

1. When [Anu] heard [these thin]gs,
2. [. . . . in the wr]ath of his heart
3. [. . . .] he sends out a messenger.
4. [. . . . But Ea, who] knows the heart of the great gods
5. [And who] sees through [the plans of the go]ds,
6. [Before] the arrival [of the messenger of Anu], the king,
7. [. . . .] sent word [to Adapa].
8. [Adapa came(?)] to Ea, the king.[31]

---

[28] Reading *is-sà-ku-at*, resulting either from a peculiar spelling or being a scribal error for *is-sà-ka-at*, from *sakâtu*.

[29] I.e., why has Ea given such magic power to Adapa as he has displayed in his encounter with the south wind? (cf. Th. Jacobsen in the *American Journal of Semitic Languages and Literatures*, XLVI [1929/30], 202).

[30] This fragment corresponds to ll. 12–21 of Fragment II.

[31] Anu was king of heaven, while Ea was king of the subterranean sweet waters.

9. He sent [. . . .].

10. [Then Ea, the broad] of understanding, who knows the heart of the great gods,

11. [. . . . in the ways] of heaven instructed(?) him.

12. [. . . .] he caused him to wear long hair;

13. [. . . .] . . . . he clothed him with a mourning garment.

14. [He gave him counsel], speaking (this) [wo]rd to him:

15. "[Adapa], thou must go [to Anu, the k]ing.

16. [Do not forget] the instruction, hold fast my word.

17. [When thou ascendest to heaven and] approachest the gate of Anu,

18. [Tammuz and Gizzida] will be standing [in the gate of A]nu."

(*Remainder wanting*)

FRAGMENT NO. IV

(*Beginning destroyed*)

2. [Oil] he commanded for him, and he was an[ointed].

3. [A ga]rment he commanded for him, and he was clothed.

4. [. . . .] Anu laughed aloud at the deed of Ea and [said]:

5. "Ye gods of heaven and earth, as many as there are, who has (ever) [commanded] thus?

6. His command is like the command of Anu. Who can increase (it)?"

7. [. . . . A]dapa from the horizon of heaven to the zenith of heaven

8. [. . . .] looked and beheld its awe-inspiring grandeur.

9. [Then] Anu imposed on Adapa ⌜. . . .⌝.

10. He decreed freedom from compulsory service for [the city] of Ea;[32]

11. To glorify his high priesthood unto far-away days ⌜he decreed⌝ as (his) destiny.

12. [At the ti]me that Adapa, the "seed of mankind,"[33]

---

[32] I.e., the city Eridu.

[33] From this expression some scholars have drawn the conclusion that Adapa was the ancestor of all mankind. However, that deduction is based on a misunderstanding of this phrase; for, as Jensen (in *Reallexikon der Assyriologie*, I, 33) has pointed out, these words mean simply that Adapa was of the seed of man, that he was a human being. Thus in the Code of Hammurabi (see R. F. Harper, *The Code*

13. [. . . .] victoriously broke the wing of the south wind
14. [And] ascended to heaven, and so forth,
15. It was established.³⁴ And what(soever) of ill he has brought upon men,
16. [And] the disease which he has brought upon the bodies of men,
17. These the goddess Ninkarrak³⁵ will allay.
18. [Let] the illness arise (and depart), let the disease turn aside!
19. [. . . .] . . may horror fall!
20. [. . . .] sweet sleep he shall not sleep!
21. [. . . .] . . . . joy of the heart of the people.

(Rest destroyed)

---

of Ḥammurabi, King of Babylon [Chicago and London, 1904], col. xliv, l. 48) this same term is employed to denote a human offspring, an heir. Analogous expressions are *zêr sharrûti*, the "seed of kingship or royalty," i.e., of royal seed, and *zêr shangûti*, the "seed of priesthood," i.e., of priestly descent. Other points against the view which makes Adapa the first human being can be derived from the fact that Ea created, or begot, him for the express purpose of being "a leader among mankind" and that he is represented as living among men (Fragment I:6–14).

³⁴ With the force of the tense cf. Fragment I:5–7.

³⁵ The goddess of healing.

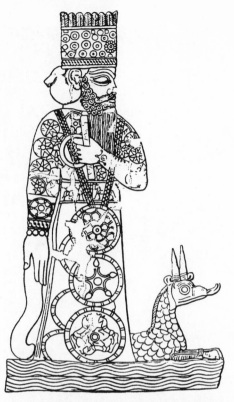

Fig. 1.—The god Marduk

Fig. 2.—A symbolical representation of the god Ashur

Fig. 3.—King Ashurbanipal, from whose library numerous fragments of *Enûma elish* have been recovered, pouring out a libation over four dead lions.

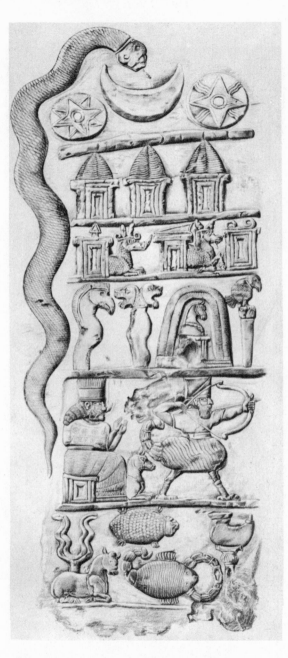

Fig. 4.—A Babylonian boundary stone of the twelfth century B.C., showing a scorpion-man in Register 5 (cf. *Enûma elish*, Tablet I:141).

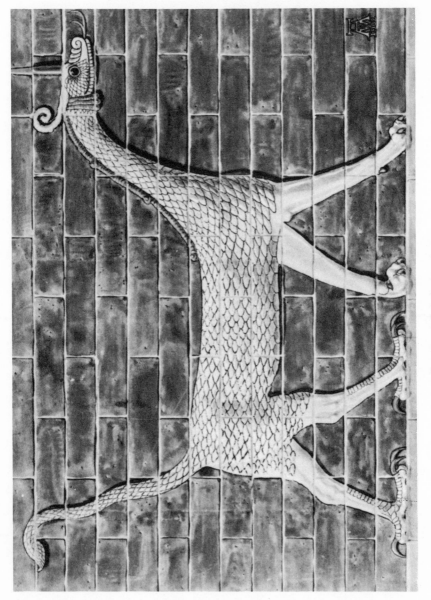

FIG. 5.—A Babylonian dragon

FIG. 6.—Fight between a god and a monster

Fig. 7.—Fight between a god and a monster. This is a drawing based upon the preceding illustration.

Fig. 8.—A seal impression depicting a fight between a god and a dragon

FIG. 9.—Part of the fourth tablet of *Enûma elish*

FIG. 10.—The sun-god appearing on the mountainous eastern horizon, with rays issuing from his shoulders and divine attendants opening the two lion-capped portals of the dawn (cf. *Enûma elish*, Tablet V:9 f.).

Fig. 11.—Restoration of the Babylon of Nebuchadrezzar (604–562 B.C.) as seen from the western bank of the Euphrates. In the foreground, opposite the city wall, is the temple complex called Esagila. To the right is the temple of Marduk and to the left the stage-tower of Marduk (cf. *Enûma elish*, Tablet VI: 45–64).

FIG. 12.—Restoration of the Babylon of Nebuchadrezzar as seen from the north end of the Procession Street, leading through the Ishtar Gate (in the foreground). To the right are the so-called "hanging gardens." In the distant background is the tower of Marduk's temple.

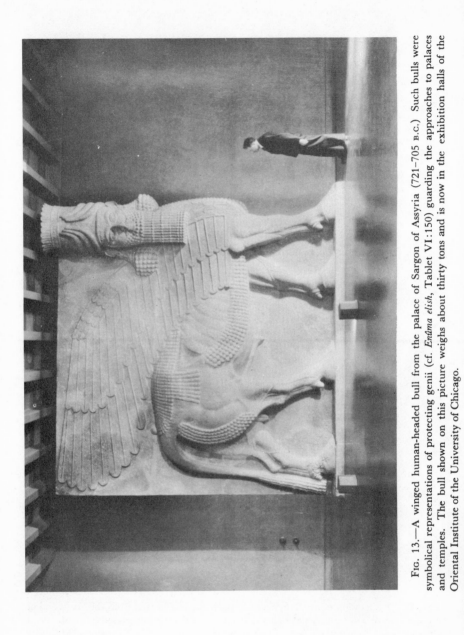

FIG. 13.—A winged human-headed bull from the palace of Sargon of Assyria (721–705 B.C.) Such bulls were symbolical representations of protecting genii (cf. *Enûma elish*, Tablet VI:150) guarding the approaches to palaces and temples. The bull shown on this picture weighs about thirty tons and is now in the exhibition halls of the Oriental Institute of the University of Chicago.

Fig. 14.—The tablet containing the bilingual version of the creation of the world by Marduk.

Fig. 15.—A seven-headed serpent on a Sumerian mace head

Fig. 16.—The slaying of a seven-headed dragon

Fig. 17.—A cylinder seal formerly supposed to represent the Babylonian tradition of the fall of man.